CW00326777

Happy Cooking

The Milestone

Derek Chapman

M.G.

FIRST CATCH YOUR PIG!

REAL COOKING WITH REAL INGREDIENTS FROM THE KITCHEN OF

THE MILESTONE

Written by:
Matt Bigland, Marc Sheldon,
Simon Ayres, James Wallis at:
The Milestone
84 Green Lane at Ball Street
Kelham Island, Sheffield S3 8SE
Telephone (0114) 272 8327

Edited by:
Martin Edwards,
Karen Horsefield, Chris Brierley
RMC Books – (0114) 250 6300

Design by:
Paul Cocker
RMC Books – (0114) 250 6300

Photography by:
Jodi Hinds – www.jodihinds.com

Contributors:
Ben Fowler, Victoria Philpott,
Max Feetham, Elaine Wallis

THE MILESTONE

First Published in 2010 on behalf of:
The Milestone
www.the-milestone.co.uk

RMC BOOKS

Published by:
RMC Books – www.rmcbooks.co.uk

CONTENTS

STARTERS

MAIN COURSES

DESSERTS

BASIC RECIPES

Acknowledgments

Firstly, we would like to thank our parents for their unconditional love and support!

Matt would particularly like to thank my beautiful wife Nina for believing in The Milestone from the very beginning and putting up with the daily dramas thrown up by the business that often pulls me away from family life. For that you're amazing!

The team, without them none of this would be possible. For coming in every day with passion and belief in the brand and for creating chaos on every staff night out - we love you all!

Special thanks goes to our senior chefs Simon Ayres and James Wallis, who helped shape this book and the journey we have all been on together which has made us who we are today. As Gordon Ramsay said; "Four Yorkshire young guns!" The intensity of Ramsay's Best Restaurant made us closer. We thank you for being fantastic friends, as well as colleagues.

We would also like to say a big thank you to our maintenance manager who comes in every Saturday and gives everything but asks for nothing except a cup of tea, a bacon butty and some lively banter... "What's happening??!!"

Finally, we'd especially like to thank our loyal guests who have seen The Milestone evolve over the last 4 years. We thank you all for your support and valuable feedback, without you we would not be where we are today!

We look forward to what the future holds- it's shit or bust!

Lots of love

Matt 'Biggi' Bigland & Marc 'Bulldog' Sheldon x

Introduction

We think Mrs Beeton would have approved.

In borrowing and adapting one of her most famous phrases as the title of this book, we touched on something both we and the great-grandma of cooking believe in.

Back in Mrs B's day, cooking meant being close to the raw ingredients. There was no supermarket, no supply chain, and no wholesaler. You either grew or reared them, or you went to the local market and squeezed, tasted and haggled over them. It's something we have lost, and it's an issue that matters to us at The Milestone.

So, as well as tried-and-tested recipes from our kitchens, the following pages say a lot about a principle we take seriously.

Mixing heritage with modernity is the driving force at The Milestone. Housed in the oldest industrial site in Sheffield, we serve dishes that stir up memories and awaken the taste buds. In our Victorian pub we resurrect the best of the old and marry it with the new, just like the listed building which we chose to realise our vision, once forgotten and derelict, now brought lovingly back to life.

The hero of The Milestone story is, of course, our food and we take meticulous care to source it locally – or create it ourselves. We use the freshest vegetables – from local allotment growers when we can, pork from our own rare breed herd of pigs, meat from local farms, game from the vast moors nearby and fish from the British coast. We don't buy anything if we can make it ourselves, including bread, pasta, chutneys and ice cream.

The faster fresh food gets cooked, the better it tastes. It's not unknown for us to change the entire menu if we have an unexpected delivery of outstanding meat or vegetables. Once we spent a whole night preparing mackerel that had been line-caught by the grandad of one of our staff. Another day we downed tools to pluck two pheasants brought in by a local farmer. It's a privilege to be able to use such quality food; we deliver its unique flavour fresh on the plate, just as it's supposed to taste.

BAR
BAR
RESTAURANT
RESTAURANT
THE MILESTONE
THE MILESTONE
THE MILESTONE
MICHELIN
2010

There's been a lot of swagger in the restaurant industry about using seasonal, local produce, but at The Milestone we genuinely put our money where our mouth is. Every ingredient in our dishes can be traced to its source. We don't think buying food from our close surroundings is extraordinary or trendy: it just makes good sense. Our ancestors created dishes in tune with the seasons for centuries, but we've lost touch with this basic practice and sacrifice flavour for convenience. If a grower arrives at The Milestone with a car boot full of rhubarb or runner beans, we create something around those ingredients and put it straight on the menu. Nature provides when it's ready and we respect that. Our philosophy on freshness extends to the meats we use, including game in season shot by a local farmer.

We also bow to tradition in many of our cooking methods. We pride ourselves on reintroducing unloved cuts to our diners including sweetbreads, brisket, beef cheek and pig's trotters. These meats need plenty of attention and slow cooking to yield unbelievable depths of flavour and succulence.

In fact, our experience of taking our first delivery of two un-butchered pigs from our herd taught us a great lesson: to use every part of the animal from trotters to tail. That week's menu centred on pork recipes created by our chefs, some of which, like pig's head, were so popular they became regular dishes. We applied the same rules to other meats and started to run 'Nose to Tail' and fish weeks in the gastropub throughout the year. Out of these thematic menus a range of fantastic recipes was born, some of which we include in this book.

Some restaurants bring out the worst in their owners: they're stuffy and snobby, worshipping at the altar of fine dining. We're operating in Yorkshire where people aren't impressed with window-dressing if the substance isn't there. We believe people should be able to eat food of superlative quality (and plenty of it) in a relaxed atmosphere.

The pared-down chic of our upstairs restaurant provides the perfect backdrop for its menu, featuring more intricate and technique-based dishes with a large helping of playfulness. Here we can show off the talents of our chefs with beautifully cooked and presented food. In the gastropub with its cosy décor, we serve more familiar, robust dishes, but always with our trademark twist.

Cooking in your own home splits itself into roughly the same categories: we all have to prepare everyday meals, but there are times when we want to step up the effort. Whatever the level of preparation and cooking involved, we think there's something here for everyone in this book, from the no-frills basic cook to the die-hard foodie. Alongside recipes for our most popular dishes is information about sourcing, seasonality and cooking techniques.

Above all, we believe cooking should be about fun and experimentation. Our kitchen is constantly trying new things and evolving original ways to serve up the finest ingredients. The end result is subjective. That's why none of our recipes are set in stone. Just try out a recipe, give it a taste and add a bit more flavour here and there. There are no rules. Our inspiration is simple: to bring out the best from the ingredients. We hope this book enthuses you to do the same.

Marc Sheldon & Matt Bigland

The Milestone at Kelham Island

The Milestone site has housed a pub for over 170 years. It started life as The Ball Inn, set up in 1833 to cater for steelworkers at Kelham Island.

The building survived the disastrous Sheffield Flood of 1864 and went on serving local ales and food for another century. With the demise of the steel industry, the pub fell into disuse. We had the chance to buy the beautiful corner building and rescue it from obscurity and this opportunity was the impetus for starting our business.

The man-made island adjacent to The Milestone was created over 900 years ago by a mill course. Over the centuries, small workshops grew into enormous factories and huge buildings of brick, glass and steel replaced rolling green meadows. The area was the booming heart of Sheffield's early industrial revolution and The Ball Inn was one of many pubs filled with the chatter of this vibrant working community.

After years of neglect, Kelham Island is now being restored; modern housing and commercial developments sit alongside factories and light industry, including one of the oldest scissor-making firms in the country. And of course nearby Kelham Island Industrial Museum is filled with information about the history of this landmark location.

We are proud to be associated with the regeneration of an area that boasts such impressive heritage and architecture; for us, it's the perfect location to recreate a traditional venue for the modern market.

GREEN LANE

THE
MILESTONE

Teamwork

As a home cook, you have something in common with restaurant chefs like me: you're looking for inspiration. Whether you're seeking challenging recipes or want to build some basic culinary skills, there's something for you in this book. The Milestone provides the perfect environment to create imaginative dishes, thanks to the availability of fabulous seasonal ingredients and a kitchen that's constantly buzzing with new ideas. I'm fortunate to have James Wallis as a right-hand man, an excellent head chef who is alive to modern trends and new methods of presentation. His on-trend style is the perfect foil for my classically trained, old school approach. We work harmoniously, learning from one another but our techniques are different. If you're an observant diner, you'll even be able to guess which chef was responsible for the way your food looks on the plate in the restaurant.

This book, like our kitchen, is a fusion of the old and the new, containing the most popular recipes from our menus, with the emphasis on British food using ingredients in season that are easy or fun to find.

When was the last time you nosed around the great outdoors to find something for dinner? As chefs at The Milestone, we take our remit to produce fabulous fresh food seriously. Even if that involves scouting Endcliffe Park in the summer for elderflowers to team up with crayfish in a veloute or putting on gloves to grab ingredients for a nettle and wild mushroom cannelloni. Wild garlic, chickweed, girolles, sweet cicely, sorrel and flowers all find their way into our dishes throughout the warmer months when nature gives generously. But you needn't go far afield to find exciting produce; it can start on your own doorstep.

BAR
BAR
THE
MILESTONE

A burgeoning number of gardeners grow their own, from simple stuff like beans, peas, herbs and potatoes to greenhouse-dependent salad leaves, tomatoes and courgettes. We're always happy for new growers to get in touch and at the moment we're looking for a local mushroom forager.

Not everyone has the time, space or inclination to grow vegetables, but if you want to ensure the best flavour, buy fruit and veg in season at your greengrocer's or farmers' market, that way you're experiencing food as it's intended to taste. Nothing beats a fresh tomato soup or consomme, oozing with an evocative summer greenhouse aroma. Great tomatoes, berries, and orchard fruits may not be available all year round, but like British asparagus, garden peas, strawberries, salad leaves and crunchy radishes, they are worth waiting for. The same principle applies to the meats we use, whether from our own herd of pigs, newly-shot game or chicken, beef and lamb from local farmers, we give every cut the time it needs to be hung, cured or cooked in a way guaranteed to maximise taste.

Another golden rule in The Milestone kitchen is that nothing ever goes to waste, so in times of plenty, fruit and veg surplus is used to create stock or make chutneys, jams and pickles.

Our prudent attitude to food is best exemplified by the way we use more unusual parts of the animal and couch unfamiliar cuts in recognisable dishes. For example, we make a cottage pie made with sweetbreads rather than beef mince; cod cheek with chips and cannelloni with pheasant breast, rabbit leg and pig's tail. We've been enormously successful in reintroducing unloved cuts and offal because our recipes make them the champions of the plate, rather than the Cinderellas of the kitchen. A quick chat with your butcher and a bit of confidence is all you need to cook these meats in your own kitchen.

Even familiar staples like roast chicken can provide up to five meals if used wisely. Most people get their bird out of the oven, carve it badly then throw the carcass away, rather than using surplus leg and wing meat for rissoles, stirfries or curries and boiling the bones for a brilliant stock. We've scattered our recipes with canny tips to getting the most out of your food, in terms of flavour and value for money.

We enjoy producing and cooking new recipes, but we couldn't have developed our repertoire without the rest of the kitchen team. We can afford to be innovative because we have a dependable, enthusiastic crew around us who take the preparation of completely novel dishes in their stride.

This book is guided by our own cooking principles, while remaining conscious of your more limited time in the kitchen and access to ingredients. From simple everyday meals to more technique-based feasts, we hope our book will make cooking more enjoyable, responsible – and fun.

Senior Head Chef Simon Ayres and the team at The Milestone

Hand reared

T A friend and I regularly met for Saturday breakfast at various cafés and restaurants around Sheffield and we always ended up bemoaning the poor quality of the meat on our plates. I decided I could probably do a better job myself and hit on the idea of rearing my own pigs to guarantee decent sausages, bacon and other cuts. It might sound a bit extreme, but pigkeeping turned into an absorbing hobby over time. I went into partnership with a friend, Andrew Hardman, who owns an arable farm at Grenoside, and Andrew's sister Wendy Duggan.

We did some research which led us to the Godfather of pigkeeping, Tony York. Tony is the oracle on pigs and lectures on them to the Royal Veterinary College. We went on one of his weekend courses in Wiltshire to find out how to set ourselves up properly, manage the pigs and keep them healthy.

After that it was a case of building the pens, registering with DEFRA and the local authority and finding some piglets. We started with 7 at first and over the past couple of years that number has fluctuated up to 15. We get the piglets when they've been weaned naturally at about 8 weeks (by comparison, commercial pigs are taken from their mothers at just 3 weeks). We feed them on barley porridge, and slightly overripe fruit and vegetables from the local post office. Their favourites are strawberries and bananas.

There are so many different breeds of pigs; we've kept Large Blacks, Oxford Sandy and Black and Berkshires, but our favourites are probably Gloucester Old Spots, a rare breed with enormous floppy ears. They have great personalities and are very tame; they never try to bite and roll over on their backs for you to scratch them.

Historically, Gloucester Old Spots roamed orchards, feeding on windfalls and folklore has it that their spots are bruises caused from falling apples. Above all, they produce excellent quality pork.

Our pigs are slaughtered at 26 weeks for pork and leaner cuts and at 35 weeks for bacon, ham and gammon. That's because in those 9 weeks, pigs lay down from 30-50lb and their meat changes subtly in flavour. We don't artificially fatten our pigs by giving them growth hormones and they're free to roam around and exercise. For that reason, they take twice as long to reach weight as commercially reared pigs, but our meat is leaner and much more tasty than anything you'd get in a supermarket.

We don't sell our meat to anyone apart from family and friends. Our connection with The Milestone began as I'm a regular customer and think it's one of the best restaurants in Sheffield. I had a good idea they'd be interested in our small operation because locally produced free-range pork ties in perfectly with their ethos. The owners Matt and Marc were impressed with our set up and could see our pigs were living the high life. What's more, the pork these pigs produce is second to none. Now we rear pigs for the restaurant according to their requirements.

We didn't intend to breed pigs here, but it's the next obvious step. We put our two gilts (virgin female pigs) with a hired boar recently and are hoping for litters from them in the near future. We've looked into different breeding and rearing methods and recently spent time at Chatsworth Farm to see their very successful programme.

In the meantime we continue to buy weaners from all over the country. We've travelled from County Durham to Lincolnshire and Selby to pick up the best piglets we can find.

I could go on. It's a funny thing, but get two pig farmers together and they'll talk about nothing else. We're just delighted we can go somewhere in Sheffield for a full English that's perfection on a plate.

Max Feetham

Everything but the oink!

Our love affair with pigs and their meat started thousands of years ago. The first domesticated pigs, probably related to wild boars, can be traced back to 5000 BC in the Near East and China. Their popularity spread thanks to the fact they were easy to keep, ate up scraps and most importantly every part of them could be eaten. Nowadays their meat is the most commonly consumed worldwide and features in different guises across global cuisine, from red roasted Asian pork to Italian pancetta and salamis, Spanish chorizo to our own bacon, sausages and roasts.

In England before the Industrial Revolution, almost every home would keep its own pig. It would be fattened up through spring and summer before being slaughtered and eaten throughout the autumn and winter. Pig by-products including lard and preserved meats like bacon, ham and gammon would be prepared through the cold months so a family could live off its pig for an entire year.

Commercial production and refrigeration mean that for the last century we've eaten pork throughout the year, but flavour and quality have suffered. Thankfully the tide is turning as more people are returning to traditional methods of pig rearing or even starting to keep pigs for the first time. In fact in the five years up to 2008, the number of smallholdings keeping fewer than ten fattening pigs rose by 32 percent. Rare breed pigs are enjoying a revival as, although they take longer to mature than breeds chosen for intensive, commercial farming, their meat is considered far superior.

In tandem with this, forgotten cuts have become more popular and once again diners can experience the unique tastes offered by different parts of the animal. We've had an adventure with our Nose to Tail weeks, which all started when we took delivery of the first pigs from our own herd. We want to share our journey of discovery that resulted in a new world of cooking – using everything but the oink!

Cuts of pork

Most of these cuts can be supplied by your local butcher. He'll also give you guidance on cooking times and methods. Try something new and surprise yourself:

HEAD: This can be delicious if cooked the right way. If you're not up for it yourself, ask your butcher to bone and tie the head before preparing it for slow cooking in a pot of stock. Also use for brawn, stocks and soups.

CHEEK: A beautifully tender cut of meat that has become a favourite in our kitchen.

EARS: So long consigned to use as dog treats, these are delicious fried and baked after boiling.

SHOULDER: Cubed shoulder pork is great for casseroles, stews and curries. For roasting, buy shoulder joint (which can be boned and rolled) and knuckle/shank for slow roasting; spare rib joint, mini collar joint and collar joint for roasting or slow cooking.

HAND: A less commonly known and cheaper cut of pork, which is good for burgers or slow braising.

LOIN: This cut from along the pig's back provides particularly fine joints (boned and rolled loin joint or loin rack joint) for roasting. A variety of steaks can be cut from the loin including: loin eye, Valentine steak (shaped like a heart) and loin steaks for frying or griddling.

BELLY: Pork belly loves marinades and stuffing prior to slow roasting. Cuts include rustic belly (with criss-cross scored fat) and rolled belly joints, large and mini belly slices and spare ribs.

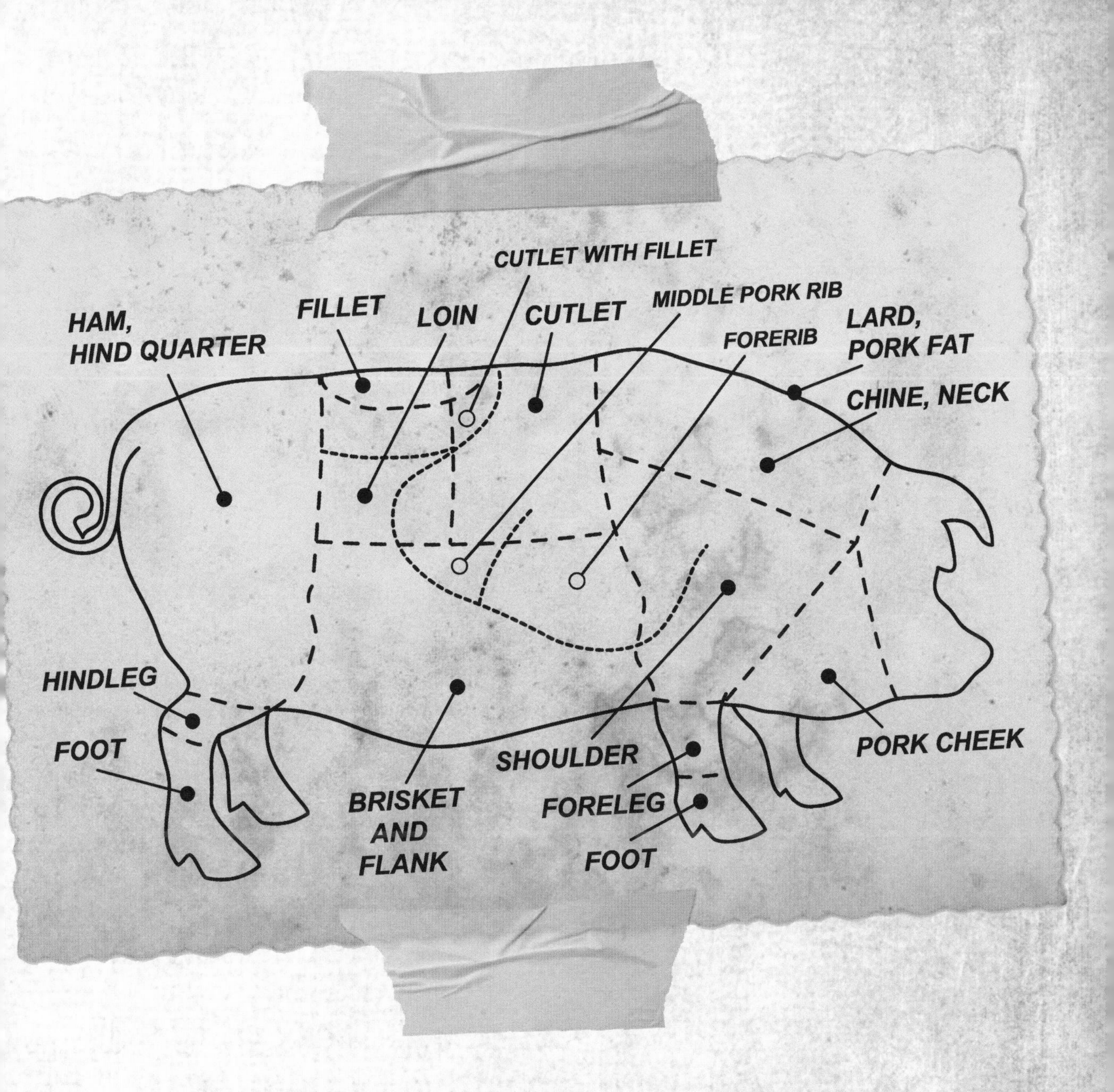

LEG: This provides the meatiest cuts. Leg joints and cushion leg joints are perfect for roasting with crispy crackling. Ham, leg steaks, and pork bucco also derive from the leg joint.

TENDERLOIN: A cut taken from the top of the back, this cut is renowned for its succulence and superb quality. Provides lean pieces for roasting whole or medallions for poaching and griddling.

CHUMP: Best known for providing chump steaks, this cut comes from where the back meets the leg. Also gives a fantastic joint to roast.

TROTTERS AND HOCKS: Usually cooked in soups or stews, this part of the pig is tasty and cheap to buy.

TAIL: Another forgotten part of the pig, the tail has long had a place in many world cuisines and is making a revival in British cooking.

LIVER, KIDNEY, HEART, TONGUE: Pork offal is incredibly delicious and features in a variety of dishes in The Milestone.

Fair game

To chefs, autumn is more about birds dropping from the sky than colourful leaves. This is the time when the shooting season begins in earnest and game from the nearby Peak District finds its way to The Milestone's kitchen. Not only is this bounty truly delicious, it's also free-range, organic, local and very fresh.

The aptly named Ben Fowler provides us with all our game requirements, from rabbit and wild duck to pheasant and woodpigeon.

All game is seasonal to an extent. Even birds you always see around like woodpigeon are agricultural pests and culled more at harvest time. Woodpigeon, as the name suggests, roost in trees and woodland, but fly into the open fields to feed on barley, oil seed, rape and wheat. Unlike their city-dwelling cousins, they enjoy a fabulous diet that makes them so tasty, but damages crops. From the end of July to the beginning of April we shoot them on their feeding grounds in farmers' fields using decoys like plastic and rubber pigeons, dead birds or sometimes a rocking cradle to create movement and attract live woodpigeons to them.

Like woodpigeon, pheasant live in woodland areas. They tend to keep undercover so the shoot uses a team of beaters and dogs to flush them into the open and drive them over 'the guns' outside the wood. We wait until we can see sky before shooting them high overhead, aiming between 10 and 2 on a clockface. Although the majority of pheasants are reared and released for shooting, there are some wild ones around in the countryside.

The season for wild duck or mallard is from September 1 to the end of January. These birds live on large lakes or reservoirs during the day, but fly to smaller ponds to feed and roost at dusk. We scatter barley around ponds and wait for the ducks to come, shooting them as they fly in. We also shoot mallard over farmers' fields, where they too can damage crops prior to the harvest. We only use non-toxic shots for duck to protect the waterways. All game birds are retrieved by our gundogs and placed on a game cart before being taken back and hung in fridges for up to 12 days for tenderising. In times gone by, game was hung by its neck until the body dropped off, but our modern stomachs probably couldn't cope with that!

We tend to ferret for rabbits from October 1 when they have stopped breeding, the young are big enough to be caught and the foliage is less dense, making it easier to spot their holes. We block the exits with nets and send ferrets into the warren complex, trapping them as they bolt. We don't shoot the rabbits, but dispatch them immediately. Some people send lurchers or greyhounds after rabbits, but that can only be effective in large areas of open land. On an average ferreting trip we will catch around 30 wild rabbits, ridding farmers of a nuisance and providing great meat for The Milestone. We don't catch hare locally, as there's such a small population here it wouldn't be sustainable; most hare comes from Lincolnshire.

Everything we hunt is sold to local restaurants or eaten ourselves, unlike the kill from big commercial or recreational shoots that often goes to waste.

In lots of ways shooting is a job that has to be done to help farmers. I've been shooting since I was 14 and I still love going out, whatever the weather. Sometimes I come back empty-handed and in that respect it's a little like fishing. The big difference is I can never lie about the size of the pigeon I shot.'

Ben Fowler

…*with respect*

At The Milestone, we look forward to the cornucopia of game arriving during the season. Wildfowl and rabbits are naturally active over large areas so their meat is very lean compared to commercially-reared animals that don't have to forage for food and have no natural predators.

When cooking game, we keep things as basic as possible so the distinctive taste of the meat can speak for itself. All the flavour is in the juices, so it is better cooked rare otherwise the tight protein can become liver-like and tough. We like to use sweet embellishments such as chocolate, fruits, root vegetables and legumes to counterbalance the succulent, earthy quality of the meat. We team duck with rhubarb, pigeon pie with peas, venison with chocolate or redcurrants and rabbit with carrot purée and braised lettuce.

We looked back through history for recipe ideas to when game was more commonly eaten. We have built an exciting repertoire of cooking methods for our special game weeks at the restaurant. We also use offal from game such as minced venison heart and rabbit liver. Not only are these cuts incredibly tasty, they cost a fraction of the price of the actual meat.

We run special game weeks throughout the shooting season, introducing our customers to a truly sumptuous riot of flavours. That said, even simple dishes like pigeon pie have become incredibly popular.

People find it hard to conceptualise how a feathery bird or furry rabbit can become a beautiful dish on the plate. That's because we've lost our connection with the journey produce makes from field to fork. It's something we keep alive at The Milestone, where respect for the seasons and our local riches is the foundation of our cooking.

Simon Ayres

Local Produce

The Milestone champions itself on working with suppliers to source ingredients that are as local as possible and to a high standard

Examples are -

Carrotts - Poskitts Farm Wakefield
Parsnips - Poskitts Farm Wakefield
New Potatoes - Holme Farm, Goldthorpe, Barnsley
Tomato - Williamson's - East Yorkshire
Herbs - Thirsk, North Yorkshire
English Onions - Harthill
Leeks, baby leeks, white, green spring cabbage - Mutton Farm, Bolsover
Asparagus - English
Strawberries - English
Milk - Newfield Dairy Mansfield

Pick of the crop

Fresh potatoes forked from the earth, cabbages prised from the soil, berries picked from bushes and apples plucked from trees. Even if you've been growing vegetables for years, there's always something miraculous about harvesting your own food. All the backbreaking work it entails has a terrific pay-off: the fabulous taste of truly fresh fruit and veg. We do everything at The Milestone to deliver that pristine flavour on a plate. And where better to source our fruit and veg than from Sheffield's finest allotment growers?

We struck on the idea some time ago when one of our customers brought in a glut of his vegetables to see if we wanted them. Not only did we accept with delight, we wanted much more. Word got around and soon we were welcoming a parade of proud growers with their premium produce into our kitchen. Whatever's in season arrives very soon after it's cropped. Our aim is always to use the fruit and veg at its freshest and we work what we're given into our menu, even if that means altering a planned dish.

In Sheffield there are plenty of people who've worked on their allotments for decades. There are many more waiting for a little patch of earth. We were amazed to learn that waiting time for the most popular allotments can be as long as 10 years. This year there are 2,300 people on Sheffield Council's waiting list, hoping for one of the mere 3,000 plots to become available. To get more 'keen-beans' digging for dinner, the council has planned five new allotment sites and is making unscheduled spot checks to identify poorly-maintained plots, which tenants might have to hand back. So start straightening up!

The Milestone has a great relationship with allotment growers in the city, who bring us their surplus in exchange for vouchers for drinks, meals or the cookery school. We receive trays of soft fruit, bunches of rhubarb, sacks of potatoes, peas, cabbages and beans of every variety. Whatever comes in finds its way to the plate very quickly, so our diners can experience that 'just picked' taste. It's a perfect arrangement that provides The Milestone with organic, local produce and those hardworking gardeners with a bit of a treat.

Britain was a nation of gardeners long before it became a nation of shopkeepers. Subsistence farming was the way of life for our sealocked ancestors. The idea of nurturing fruit and vegetables for our own consumption has become a trendy ideology, but for many years allotments provided everything for the family table.

Allotments started thousands of years ago when the Saxons cleared woods to create common land for farming. After the Norman Conquest, feudal peasants worked strips of land for the lord. In the Elizabethan era, tenants who had been dispossessed of land for enclosure were given small allotments attached to their cottages in compensation.

In the Victorian era, allotments were made available to terrace-dwelling workers in major towns to keep people fed, occupied and out of the pubs.

During and after WW2, blockades and rationing kept the demand for homegrown food high. The number of UK allotments peaked at almost 1.5 million, but steadily declined until a revival of interest in the 70s. This was in part due to TV sit-com 'The Good Life' which made viewers yearn for the self-sufficient idyll portrayed by Tom and Barbara (Richard Briers and Felicity Kendall). The programme was years ahead of its time and is still credited with inspiring many fans to start growing their own.

Demand for allotments levelled off in the 80s and 90s, then began to rise as more city-slickers resolved to cultivate their own little patch and grow 'real food'. Even the Queen recently turned over part of the palace grounds to growing fruit and vegetables for the first time since the war. Her Majesty's has some celebrity company; Jamie Oliver, Charles Dance and Radio 4's John Humphreys all keep allotments too.

James Wallis

Beetroot and vodka pickled herring, a dill Martini, beetroot salad and horseradish crème fraîche

Ingredients

FOR THE HERRING:

4 fillets herring

100ml vodka

200g raw beetroot, grated

150ml white wine vinegar

100g caster sugar

1 teaspoon coriander seeds

1 teaspoon fennel seeds

150g Maldon sea salt

TO MAKE A BEETROOT SALAD:

2 beetroots (we use candy stripe and yellow)

FOR HORSERADISH CRÈME FRÂICHE

100g crème frâiche

1 tablespoon horseradish sauce

Juice of half a lemon

TO MAKE A DILL MARTINI:

75ml Noilly Prat

75ml vodka

Large handful dill

Juice 1 lemon

25ml sugar syrup (made from equal quantities of sugar and water brought to the boil and then simmered until thickened slightly)

Method

For the herring:

Ensure the herring is free from any pinbones and then place on a plastic tray with the Maldon sea salt covering it. Cover with cling film and place in the fridge for 3 hours to help cure and firm up the fish.

Wash off the salt under cold running water and then pat dry with kitchen roll.

To make the pickle, place the vodka, caster sugar, vinegar, coriander seeds and fennel seeds in a saucepan and then bring to the boil. Allow to cool and add the grated beetroot.

Blend in a liquidiser into a fine purée.

Place the herring in the cool pickle and allow to cure for 24 hours.

Remove the herring from the pickle and then pat dry with kitchen roll. Slice each fillet into three portions and reserve for plating.

For the beetroot salad:

Cook the beetroot, boil in their skins until soft. Peel and then cut into 1cm cubes.

To make the horseradish crème frâiche:

Mix all the ingredients together and leave to infuse for an hour, then pass through a fine sieve.

Dill Martini:

Add all the ingredients into a cocktail shaker with ice and then shake for 10 seconds, strain and discard the ice and dill.

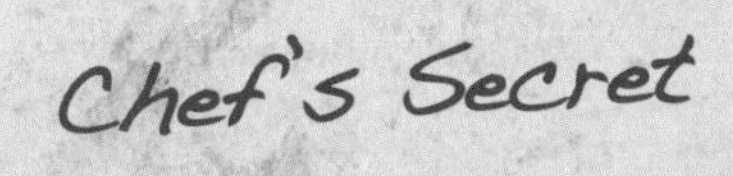

Chef's Secret

Make sure you use raw uncooked beetroot for the herring, otherwise you will not achieve the brilliant magenta colour.

Black pudding, home cured bacon, fried quail's egg and Bloody Mary

Ingredients

Quail eggs, one per person

FOR THE BLACK PUDDING:

1 litre fresh pig's blood

1 onion, finely chopped

1 clove garlic

12 sage leaves, finely chopped

125g pork back fat, cut into 1cm cubes

75g sultanas

75g pearl barley, boiled until soft

75g porridge oats

Pinch white pepper

FOR THE BACON:

1 pork belly rib, bones removed

500g sea salt

250g caster sugar

2 star anise, crushed

5 cloves

FOR THE BLOODY MARY:

50ml vodka

200ml tomato juice

Pinch salt and pepper

2 dashes tabasco

Half a lemon, juiced

Method

To make the black pudding:

Blend the blood with a stick blender until smooth.

Pass through a fine sieve.

Cook the onion, garlic and sage until soft.

Add the remaining ingredients and cook over a low heat for 10-15 minutes.

Place the mix in a terrine mould lined with baking parchment and bake in a bain marie at 120ºc for 45 minutes.

Check the black pudding is cooked by placing a knife into the centre of the pudding. If clean, the pudding is cooked.

Remove from the oven and allow to cool.

To cure the bacon:

Mix ingredients and rub onto the pork.

Place on a plastic tray.

Cover and refrigerate for 5 days.

Wash the curing mixture off the meat and pat dry.

Slice with a meat slicer or sharp knife.

Lay the rashers on a flat baking tray, place another tray on top and bake at 170ºc for 5-10 minutes until crisp.

For the Bloody Mary:

Mix ingredients with ice and strain.

Serve in shot glasses.

To assemble:

Pan-fry the quail eggs.

Pan-fry the black pudding in a little oil and top with the egg and bacon.

Serve with the Bloody Mary.

Butternut squash and orange risotto

Ingredients

200g risotto rice (we use Arborio)
Half litre vegetable stock, (hot)
1 large butternut squash
1 small bunch of parsley, finely chopped
1 small bunch of tarragon, finely chopped
1 small onion, finely diced
85g Parmesan
50g butter
1 large orange

Method

To make the butternut purée:

Wrap the butternut squash in tinfoil and roast at 170ºc for 1 hour.

Remove from the oven and allow to cool. Cut in half and remove seeds.

Scoop out the flesh and discard the skin and the seeds.

Place the flesh in a food processor with 25g of the butter and blend to a smooth purée.

Reserve until finishing the risotto.

For the risotto:

In a pan large enough to cook the rice, sweat the onions in a small amount of vegetable oil until soft and translucent.

Stir in the rice ensuring you coat all the grains. Pour on the white wine and reduce until almost disappeared, then cover with 2 ladles of the vegetable stock.

Cook until nearly absorbed and repeat until all the stock is gone and the rice is al dente.

Stir through the purée (you will probably need only half or so), and add the orange segments, Parmesan and butter. Season with salt and serve.

Curried cauliflower soup

Chef's Secret

This is a wonderful warming soup for winter, the curry powder gives an aromatic warming kick.

Ingredients

2 heads cauliflower, cut into florets
1 onion, peeled and chopped
2 cloves garlic
1 teaspoon mild curry paste
1 teaspoon garam masala
2 pints milk
1 red chilli, chopped and de-seeded

Method

Cook the onion, garlic, curry paste, chilli and garam masala in a teaspoon of oil until soft.

Pour in the milk and bring to the boil.

Add the cauliflower and simmer for 10 minutes.

Place in a liquidiser and blend to a fine purée.

Season with salt and pass through a sieve.

Ideal served with fresh homemade bread, see our recipe on page 159.

Milestone fish fingers in beer batter

Ingredients

FOR THE FISH FINGERS:

400g white fish, cut into fingers (Pollock, Coley or Cod are ideal)

FOR THE BATTER:

200g plain flour

350g beer

100g cornflour

1 egg yolk

FOR THE MUSHY PEAS:

200g frozen peas

50g butter

Handful of mint leaves

Method

For the fish fingers:

First roll the fish in the flour, then the egg and finally the breadcrumbs.

Deep fry at 180ºc for 4-5 minutes or until golden and the fish is cooked through.

To make the mushy peas:

Blanch the peas for 30 seconds in a pan of boiling water and then place into a food processor.

Add the butter and mint and pulse until a thickish consistency.

Serve with a wedge of lemon and some tartar sauce.

Chef's Secret

Perfect comfort food. Everyone's favourite and guaranteed no added e-numbers or minced up fish trimmings!

It's the reel thing
Fishing

Red mullet terrine with wasabi mayonnaise and caper dressing

Ingredients

1kg fresh red mullet fillets, pin boned and descaled
1 leek (use only the white part)

FOR THE DRESSING:
30g caperberries in brine
50ml olive oil
Juice of 1 lemon
Handful of finely chopped parsley

FOR THE WASABI MAYONNAISE:
2 medium egg yolks
25ml white wine vinegar
1 teaspoon wasabi paste
300ml light olive oil
Good squeeze fresh lemon juice
1 teaspoon lecithin powder
1 tablespoon water

Method

Cut the root off the leek and then thoroughly wash the leek in cold water.

Place the leek in a large pan of boiling water for 10 seconds to soften and then place in cold iced water to refresh and stop cooking.

Gently pan-fry the mullet in a small amount of oil until cooked through.

Line a terrine mould with cling film and then add a layer of the leeks. Allow a small amount of overlap on the cling film to finish the terrine.

Fill the terrine with the mullet and then seal the cling film.

Place a heavy weight on top of the terrine and press in the fridge for 24 hours.

Once set, cut into 1.5cm slices. Take great care in doing this as the terrine is quite delicate.

How to make the mayonnaise:
Sit a large bowl on a cloth to stop it moving.

Put the egg yolks, vinegar and lecithin into the bowl and whisk well until smooth.

Tip: You can also make this in a food processor, adding the oil through the feeder tube. It will keep in the fridge for 3-4 days.

Gradually add the olive oil in a slow, steady stream, whisking all the time. You should have a smooth, quite thick mayonnaise that stands in peaks.

Add the water and wasabi paste then add the lemon juice to taste and briefly whisk.

For the dressing:
Drain the capers from the brine and pan-fry until crisp then mix all the remaining ingredients together.

Chef's Secret
This is a really great way to enjoy fresh fish. If you prefer you can swap the wasabi mayonnaise for horseradish mayonnaise.

Ox tongue fritters & sweet chilli jam

Don't let the cat get your tongue! This dish isn't as daunting in preparation as you might think, and the rich, robust flavour of the meat is well worth it.

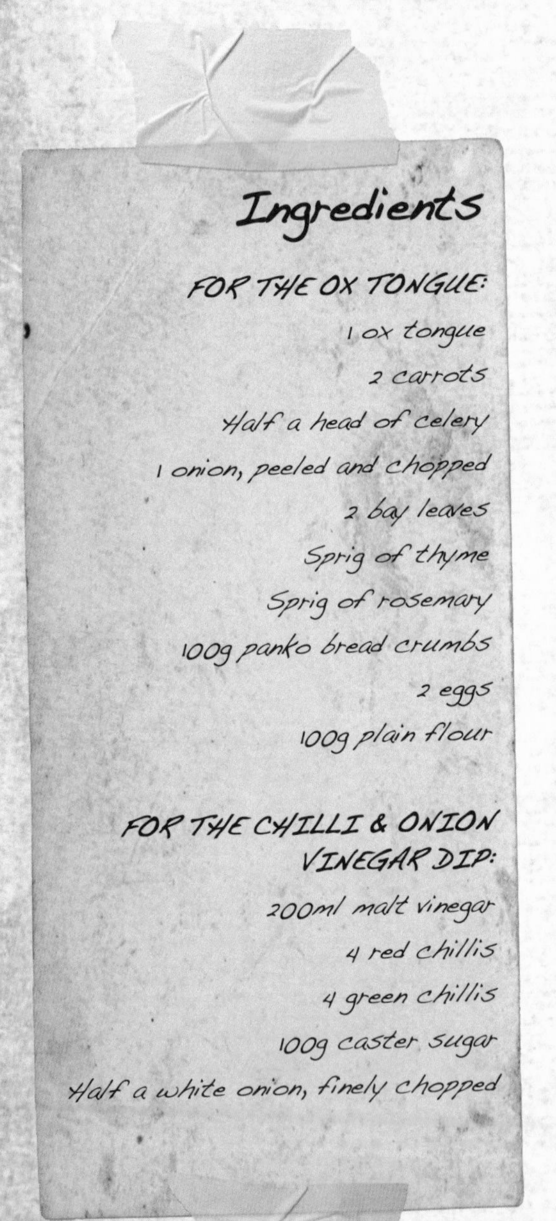

Method

For the ox tongue:

Place the ox tongue in cold water and bring to the boil. Once it starts to boil, refresh under cold running water.

Repeat the process once more. This removes any scum and bitterness from the ox tongue.

On the third boil add all the vegetables and aromatics, then simmer for three hours until the ox tongue is tender.

Remove from the liquid. When it is cool enough to handle peel away the tough outer layer of the tongue.

Chop the tongue into cubes and place through a meat mincer. If you do not have one put it through a food processor and the texture will still be acceptable.

Place the tongue mince into a tray lined with parchment, place another sheet on top and then weigh down with another tray. Press down firmly and leave to set in the fridge.

Once set, cut into 1 inch cubes ready for the crumbs.

To breadcrumb the meat, roll the cubes through the flour, then the beaten egg and then the panko breadcrumbs.

Deep fry at 180ºc until golden and crisp.

For the chilli dip:

Place all the ingredients in a saucepan and boil until reduced by half. Allow to cool and serve with the fritters.

Chef's Secret

Try to get Japanese panko breadcrumbs, they're made from bread without crusts, and have a crisper texture than normal breadcrumbs.

Pea pannacotta, shoots, seeds, soil and flowers

Chef's Secret

You can buy sprouting beans from health food shops, which is a lot easier than sprouting your own!

Ingredients

FOR THE PANNACOTTA:

400g peas

2g agar agar powder (if not vegetarian gelatine can be substituted use 4 leaves soaked in cold water)

FOR THE SOIL:

200g black olives

Tablespoon of water

FOR THE GARNISH:

Handful pea shoots

25g mixed seeds (we use sesame, sunflower and linseed)

25g sprouting shoots

Small handful of edible flowers i.e nasturtiums, pansies, rose or violet

Method

To make the pannacotta:

Bring a large pan of water to the boil and blanch the peas until soft. Blend the peas with a small amount of the cooking liquor and then pass though a fine strainer.

Add a small amount of the cooking liquor until you have a pint of purée.

Chill in a metal bowl over another bowl filled with ice. This cools the purée quickly and retains the bright green colour.

Season with salt to taste.

Bring a small amount of the liquid to the boil and whisk in the agar agar powder, add the remaining pea purée and then set in dariole moulds in the fridge.

To turn out, dip the mould into boiling water for 1 second to loosen the pannacotta.

For the soil:

Place the black olives in a blender with a tablespoon of water and blend to a smooth purée.

To assemble:

Place the pannacotta on the plate and make a 'path' with the seeds. Spread the 'soil' on the plate, and scatter a few pea shoots around.

Pigeon black pudding salad with sloe gin dressing

Ingredients

4 pigeon breasts
100g watercress

FOR THE BLACK PUDDING:

1 litre fresh pig's blood
1 onion, finely chopped
1 clove garlic
12 sage leaves, finely chopped
125g pork back fat, cut into 1cm cubes
75g sultanas
75g pearl barley, boiled until soft
75g porridge oats
Pinch white pepper

SLOE GIN DRESSING:

1 egg yolk
100ml vegetable oil
30ml white wine vinegar
25ml sloe gin
2 juniper berries, ground to a powder
Pinch of salt

Method

For the dressing:

Whisk the egg yolk and vinegar until light, fluffy and doubled in size.

Slowly pour in the vegetable oil, whisking at all times so the dressing does not split.

Repeat the process with the sloe gin, then add the ground juniper berries.

Season with salt.

To make the black pudding:

Blend the blood with a stick blender until smooth.

Pass through a fine sieve.

Cook the onion, garlic and sage until soft.

Add the remaining ingredients and cook over a low heat for 10-15 minutes.

Place the mix in a terrine mould lined with baking parchment and bake in a bain marie at 120ºc for 45 minutes.

Check the black pudding is cooked by placing a knife into the centre of the pudding. If clean, the pudding is cooked.

Remove from the oven and allow to cool.

To assemble:

Pan-fry the pigeon breast and the black pudding (we serve the pigeon pink but cook according to your own preference).

Toss the spinach leaves in a small amount of the dressing.

Place the salad in a bowl, top with the a slice of black pudding and then the pigeon.

Drizzle the remaining dressing over the pigeon and serve.

Pigeon pudding and pea purée

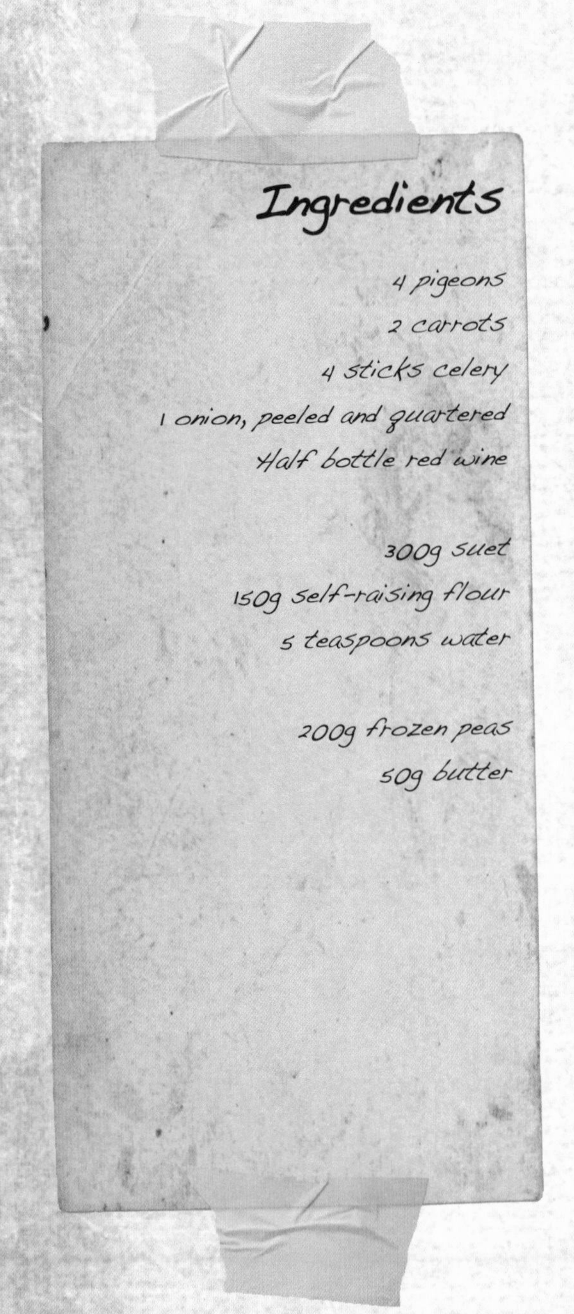

Method

For the pigeons:

In a hot pan, colour the pigeons all over with a small amount of vegetable oil. Remove from the pan and set aside. Add the vegetables and colour. Pour in the red wine and reduce by two thirds.

Place the pigeons and vegtables in a deep ovenproof dish. Cover with cold water then seal with tin foil and place in a pre-heated oven at 140°c. Braise for 3 hours.

Once tender, remove the pigeons from the liquor and leave until cool enough to handle. Pick all the meat from the birds, ensuring no bones remain. Pass the cooking liquor through a fine sieve, skim the stock of any fat and scum and reduce to an intensely-flavoured sauce. Combine the sauce and the shredded pigeon meat.

To make the suet paste:

Sieve the flour into a large electric mixing bowl. Add the suet and water and mix on a medium speed until the fat is incorporated into the flour and a smooth dough is formed. Allow the dough to rest in the fridge for 30 minutes.

For the pea purée:

Blanch the peas in a large pan of salted boiling water, then place in a liquidiser and blend until smooth. Add the butter to help emulsify and then pass through a fine sieve. Season with salt and set aside.

To make the puddings:

Lightly coat the inside of small dariole moulds or steamproof earthenware dishes with butter. Roll out the pastry to the thickness of a pound coin and then line the moulds. Spoon in the filling. When almost full, place another disc of the pastry on top and seal with water.

Place the puddings in a steamer for 45 minutes - 1 hour. Turn out the puddings immediately and serve with the heated pea purée.

Home cured bacon, asparagus and poached quail eggs, truffle vinagrette

Serves 4

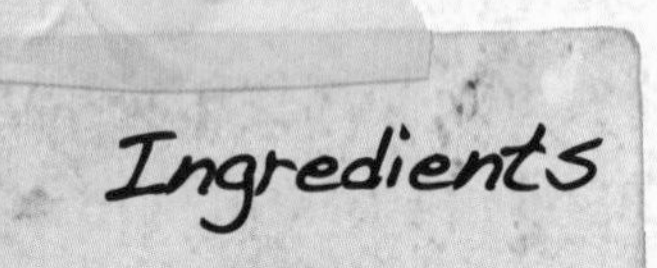

Ingredients

16 asparagus spears
12 quails' eggs

TO MAKE YOUR OWN BACON:
Half a pork belly
500g Maldon sea salt
250g caster sugar
3 cloves
1 cinnamon stick broken up
3 star anise
10 juniper berries

FOR THE MAYONNAISE:
2 medium egg yolks
25ml white wine vinegar
1 teaspoon truffle oil
300ml light olive oil
Good squeeze fresh lemon juice
1 teaspoon lecithin powder
1 tablespoon water

Method

First make the bacon in advance:

Mix all the ingredients together and then rub into the pork belly. Place on a plastic tray and then cling film tightly and refrigerate for 4 days minimum and 6 maximum, we find 5 ideal.

After 4-6 days, wash the bacon in cold water and then pat dry with kitchen roll and then freeze for two hours to firm up.

How to make the mayonnaise:

Sit a large bowl on a cloth to stop it moving.

Put the egg yolks, vinegar and lecithin into the bowl and whisk well until smooth.

Tip: You can also make this in a food processor, adding the oil through the feeder tube. It will keep in the fridge for 3-4 days.

Gradually add the olive oil in a slow, steady stream, whisking all the time. You should have a smooth, quite thick mayonnaise that stands in peaks.

Add the water and truffle oil and add lemon juice to taste then briefly whisk.

To poach the quails eggs:

Bring a pan of water to the boil and add a good splash of white wine vinegar.

Crack the quails eggs into small ramekins and discard any that have split yolks, poach for 1 minute and then refresh into cold water.

Snap the asparagus at the woody points and then peel the stems, blanch in boiling water for 20-30 seconds or until tender, then place in iced water to stop the cooking.

To make the bacon crisps:

Slice the bacon as thin as possible and then place between two layers of parchment and between two heavy baking trays, bake at 170ºc for 10-15 minutes until crisp.

To assemble:

Reheat the asparagus and quails egg in a pan of boiling water.

Place the spears on the bottom of the plate and then pour on some of the dressing. Top the asparagus with the eggs and the bacon crisps and garnish with pea shoots.

Chef's Secret

This dish is best enjoyed in the six short weeks that British asparagus is in season – a real treat, enjoy it while you can.

Salmon cured in botanicals with a cucumber, lime and Hendricks gin chilled soup

Ingredients

Half a side salmon
250g Maldon seasalt
125g caster sugar
6 juniper berries
18 coriander seeds
1 small piece of cassia bark
Quarter stick of liquorice, grated
2 lemons, zested

FOR THE CUCUMBER SOUP:

2 cucumbers, peeled and seeds removed
100ml tonic water
75ml Hendricks gin
25ml sugar syrup (equal quantities of sugar and water cooked out until slightly thickened)
Small handful of coriander leaves
Small handful of mint leaves
Juice of 1 lime

Method

To cure the salmon:

Mix all the ingredients together and then rub into the salmon. Allow to cure in the fridge, wrapped tightly in cling film, for 12 hours.

Wash the salmon in cold water and then pat dry with kitchen roll. Slice thinly (to a similar thickness to smoked salmon) and remove the dark brown meat, as this tends to be quite bitter.

For the cucumber soup:

Place all the ingredients in a liquidiser and blend until smooth. Pass through a fine sieve and season with salt.

To serve:

Place some of the salmon in a bowl and add the soup, float a few borage flowers in the soup (borage flowers are purple and have a cucumber flavour).

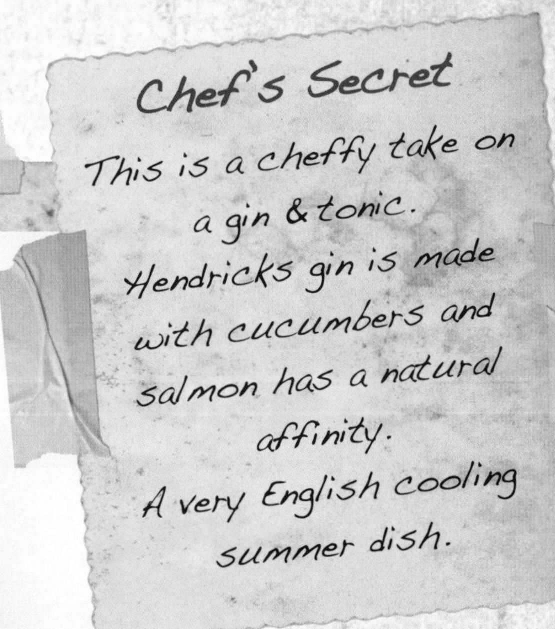
Chef's Secret
This is a cheffy take on a gin & tonic.
Hendricks gin is made with cucumbers and salmon has a natural affinity.
A very English cooling summer dish.

Hop cured salmon with local real ale

Ingredients

Half side of salmon
250g Maldon sea salt
50ml dark treacle
125g caster sugar
15g dried hops

Method

To cure the salmon:

Mix all the ingredients together and then rub into the salmon. Allow to cure in the fridge, wrapped tightly in cling film, for 12 hours.

Wash the salmon in cold water and then pat dry with kitchen roll. Slice thinly (to a similar thickness to smoked salmon) and remove the dark brown meat, as this tends to be quite bitter.

To serve:

With half a glass of Kelham Island Best Bitter but if you fancy a full pint with it… well, why not?

Chef's Secret
The hops are the perfect bitter counter balance for the rich and salty salmon. You can buy hops from any good brewers shop, or from the internet

Cured sea trout with rocket purée

Chef's Secret

The creaminess of the sea trout benefits from the peppery tang of the rocket.

Ingredients

One side of line caught sea trout
250g Maldon sea salt
125g caster sugar
100g rocket

Method

To cure the sea trout, mix all the ingredients together except the rocket and then rub into the sea trout.

Wrap the trout tightly in cling film and allow to cure in the fridge for 12 hours.

Wash the sea trout in cold water and then pat dry with kitchen roll.

Bring a large pan of water to the boil and blanch the rocket for 8 seconds to wilt it. Drain and then purée in a liquidiser. Once cool, rub all the rocket over the sea trout.

Slice thinly to a thickness of 1-2cm and remove the dark brown meat as this tends to be quite bitter.

Serve with a spoonfull of the purée and a fresh cucumber salad.

Pan-fried scallops, carpaccio of pigs head, squid and squid ink

Ingredients

4 scallops

4 baby squid tubes, cut into thin strips

Handful pea shoots (to garnish)

FOR THE PIG'S HEAD:

1 pig's head

2 carrots, peeled and chopped

4 sticks celery, peeled and chopped

1 star anise

1 onion, peeled and chopped

1 white leek

Half bottle white wine

2 cloves garlic

Water to cover

FOR THE SQUID INK PAINT:

5g squid ink

15ml vegetable oil

Method

To prepare the pig's head:

To bone the head, run a boning knife from the top of the skull, following the line of the bone closely to avoid breaking the skin.

Remove the flesh from the right hand cheek and repeat on the left.

Cut off the ears and remove any hairs with a razor or blowtorch.

Butterfly the cheek meat, cut the tongue in half and place each half in each side of the head.

Season with salt and roll tightly in cling film to maintain the shape.

Place the remaining ingredients in an ovenproof dish with a tight-fitting lid and cover with water.

Braise at 140ºc for 4-5 hours, until tender.

Remove the head from the cooking juices and allow to cool. When cool enough to handle, remove the cling film and then re-roll in more cling film, ensuring it is watertight.

Place in an ice bath to cool.

To assemble:

Whisk the squid ink and oil together.

Fry the squid over a high heat for 30 seconds.

Pan-fry the scallops for 45 seconds on each side.

Using a sharp knife, cut a thin slice of the pig's head and place on a warm plate.

Paint the squid ink onto the plate using a pastry brush, place the squid and scallops on the slice of pig's head and garnish with a few pea shoots.

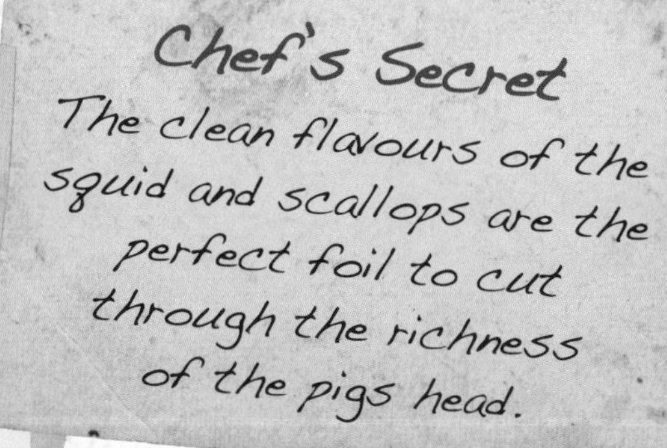
Chef's Secret
The clean flavours of the squid and scallops are the perfect foil to cut through the richness of the pigs head.

Pan-fried scallop, ox tongue corn beef and tomato fondue

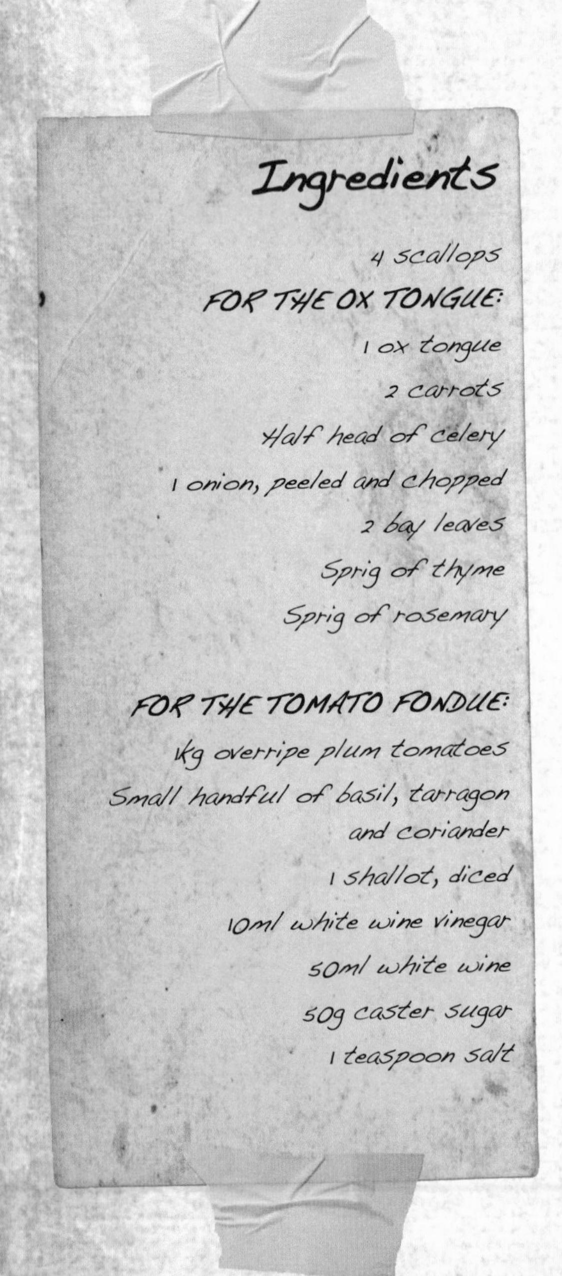

Ingredients

4 scallops

FOR THE OX TONGUE:

1 ox tongue

2 carrots

Half head of celery

1 onion, peeled and chopped

2 bay leaves

Sprig of thyme

Sprig of rosemary

FOR THE TOMATO FONDUE:

1kg overripe plum tomatoes

Small handful of basil, tarragon and coriander

1 shallot, diced

10ml white wine vinegar

50ml white wine

50g caster sugar

1 teaspoon salt

Method

For the scallops:

To remove the scallops from the shells, hold the shell open with your thumb and grip the back with your fingers. Scrape a butter knife along the flat side to release the scallop from the shell.

Remove the roe, black sac and beard from the scallop and then wash and pat dry with kitchen roll.

To make the ox tongue:

Place the ox tongue in colt water and bring to the boil. Once it starts to boil, refresh under cold running water

Repeat the process once more. This removes any scum and bitterness from the tongue

On the third boil add all the vegetables and aromatics. Simmer for 3 hours until the tongue is soft

Remove from the liquor and peel away the tough outer layer when it is cool enough to handle

Once cool, chop the tongue into cubes and place through a meat mincer. If you do not have one, put it through a food processor and the texture will still be acceptable

Place the tongue mince into a tray lined with parchment. Place another sheet on top and then another tray. Press down firmly and set in the fridge

To make the tomato fondue:

First ensure sure all equipment is particularly clean and well sanitised.

Core the tomatoes and cut into quarters.

Combine all the ingredients and leave to infuse for 3 hours.

Purée in a blender until smooth.

To assemble:

Place the ox tongue into a circle cutter and flatten.

Pan-fry the scallops for 1-2 minutes on each side.

Top the corned beef with the fondue and place the scallop on top.

Scallops with a citrus butter and lobster mayonnaise

Ingredients

12 large scallops
1 small lobster
Small handful pea shoots to garnish

FOR THE LOBSTER REDUCTION:

Reserved lobster shells
50g each of carrots, celery and onion, diced
150ml tomato juice
1-2 bay leaves
100ml white wine
50ml Noilly Prat
300ml water

FOR THE CITRUS BUTTER:

50g unsalted butter
Zest of 1 lemon and juice

FOR THE LOBSTER MAYONNAISE:

2 medium egg yolks
1 teaspoon Dijon mustard
300ml light olive oil
Squeeze fresh lemon juice
Pinch salt and pepper

Method

For the lobster:

To humanely dispatch the lobster, place in the freezer an hour before cooking. This will send the lobster to sleep by slowing its nervous system down.

Bring a large pan of salted water to the boil. Place the lobster in the water and cook for 8 minutes. Plunge into a large pan of cold iced water to immediately stop the cooking.

Remove the claws and using either a lobster cracker or the back of a heavy knife, break the claws and pick out the meat. Split the lobster in two and remove the meat from the tail then clean out the head. Reserve the shells for the lobster reduction and the meat for the mayonnaise.

For the reduction:

Place the lobster shells into a roasting tray and then roast at 190ºc for 15 minutes. Blend the lobster meat in a food processor till the meat resembles fine grains.

Meanwhile sweat the celery, onion and carrots with a teaspoon of vegetable oil. Cook until soft.

Add the wine and Noilly Prat and then reduce until almost all the liquid has cooked off.

Add the lobster shells, tomato juice and water and simmer for 1 hour.

Place the mixture (shells included) into a liquidiser and blend until really smooth.

Pass the mixture through a fine strainer and then reduce over a medium heat until 100ml is left.

For the lobster mayonnaise:

Place the egg yolks into the bowl with the Dijon mustard and a little seasoning. Whisk until smooth.

Gradually add the olive oil in a slow, steady stream, whisking constantly. You should have a smooth, thick mayonnaise that stands in peaks.

Add lemon juice to taste.

If it's too thick, whisk in a few drops of warm water to give a good consistency.

Add the chopped lobster meat and the lobster reduction and gently whisk through.

To cook the scallops:

To remove the scallops from the shells, hold the shell open with your thumb and grip the back with your fingers. Scrape a butter knife along the flat side to release the scallop from the shell.

Remove the roe, black sac and beard from the scallop and then wash and pat dry with kitchen roll.

For the citrus butter:

Place the butter, zest and juice in a food processor and cream together.

Place the butter in the fridge till ready for use.

To assemble:

Pan-fry the scallops in a hot pan for a minute or two on either side and then add the butter to the pan to coat the scallops.

Place three dollops of the mayonnaise on a plate and drag a line using the back of a spoon. Place the 3 scallops on the 3 lines of mayonnaise, pour over the butter and garnish with the pea shoots.

Sesame cured pollock with bok choi, sesame seeds and chilli salad

Ingredients

TO CURE THE POLLOCK:

400g pollock, scaled and pinboned

10ml sesame oil

200g sea salt

150g caster sugar

20g sesame seeds to garnish

FOR THE SALAD:

1 bok choi

Half red chilli, de-seeded

1 teaspoon sesame oil

1 teaspoon soy sauce

Method

To prepare the pollock:

Cover the pollock with the sesame oil, sugar and salt.

Wrap tightly in cling film and refrigerate for 4 hours.

Rinse off in cold running water and pat dry.

Rub the fish with the sesame seeds and slice wafer thin.

To make the salad:

Finely shred the bok choi and chilli and dress with sesame oil and soy sauce.

To assemble:

Lay the pollock onto a plate and top with the bok choi salad.

Drizzle the dressing around the plate.

Chef's Secret

Pollock is a great sustainable option instead of cod. If pollock is not available why not try mackerel or grey mullet.

Tomato consommé with edible soil, flowers and tomato agar

Ingredients

FOR THE CONSOMMÉ:

2kg overripe plum tomatoes

Small handful of basil, tarragon and coriander

1 shallot, diced

10ml white wine vinegar

50ml white wine

50g caster suger

1 teaspoon salt

FOR THE SOIL:

200g black olives

Tablespoon of water

FOR THE TOMATO AGAR:

200g tomato consommé

1g agar agar

TO GARNISH:

Pea shoots

Edible flowers

Method

For the consommé:

First ensure all equipment is particularly clean and well-sanitised.

Core the tomatoes and cut into quarters.

Combine all the ingredients and leave to infuse for 3 hours.

Purée in a blender until smooth.

Hang the pulp in a muslin bag and transfer to a cool place then allow the clear consommé to drip through into a container for 24 hours.

Bring the clear consommé to the boil and then correct the seasoning.

For the soil:

Place the black olives in a blender with a tablespoon of water and blend to a smooth purée.

To make the tomato agar:

Place the 200g consommé in a saucepan and bring to the boil.

Whisk in the agar agar powder and keeping whisking until fully disolved.

Pour into a small plastic container so the jelly will be 1cm thick when cut and set in the fridge.

To assemble:

Place a small plant pot or ramekin in the centre of the bowl and add your edible soil and decorative flowers.

Cut out 1cm cubes of the tomato agar agar jelly and place around the pot, then gently pour in a serving of the tomato consommé.

Chef's Secret

We serve our consommé with a plant pot and miniature watering can! In hommage to greenhouses full of ripe summer tomatoes!

Yorkshire rarebit & Milestone Bread with Henderson's Relish

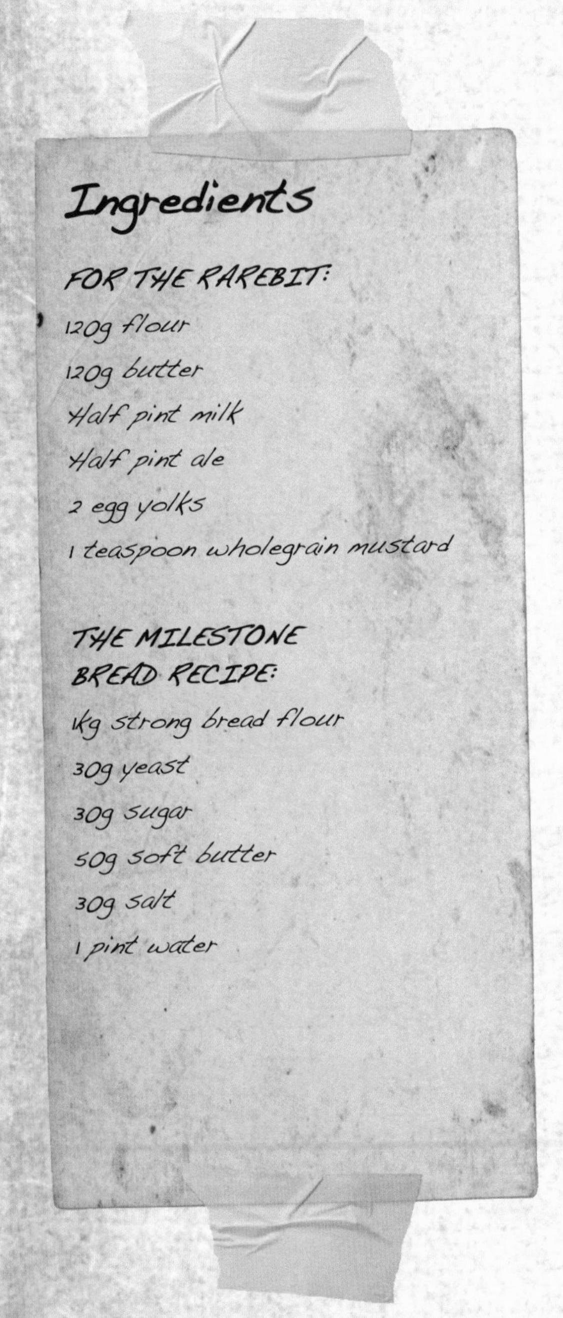

Ingredients

FOR THE RAREBIT:

120g flour

120g butter

Half pint milk

Half pint ale

2 egg yolks

1 teaspoon wholegrain mustard

THE MILESTONE BREAD RECIPE:

1kg strong bread flour

30g yeast

30g sugar

50g soft butter

30g salt

1 pint water

Method

To make the rarebit:

Melt the butter in a saucepan and add the flour, stir until mixed together into a roux.

Slowly add the milk and then bring to the boil.

After all the milk is stirred in, add the ale and cook out to a thick sauce.

Take off the heat and stir in the yolks and wholegrain mustard.

Season with salt and pepper to taste.

To finish slice 4 thick slices of bread (recipe below) and toast lightly.

Top with the rarebit and place under the grill until golden.

To bake your own Milestone Bread:

Combine the sugar, yeast, and water, then put to one side in a warm place and leave for 15 minutes.

Meanwhile, fold together the flour and salt and place in a food processor. If kneading by hand, tip the flour onto a work surface and make a well in the centre.

Add the liquid mix and the butter to the well and then mix until an elastic dough is formed.

Kneading by hand will take 10-15 minutes, if using a mixer about 5 minutes.

Cover with a clean damp cloth and then leave to prove in a warm place for 45 minutes-1 hour 30 minutes or until the dough has doubled in size.

Knead for another 5 minutes.

Cut into 2 large and 1 small loaves or into 3 for medium sized loaves.

Prove the loaves again until doubled in size.

Bake at 185ºc for 25-35 minutes.

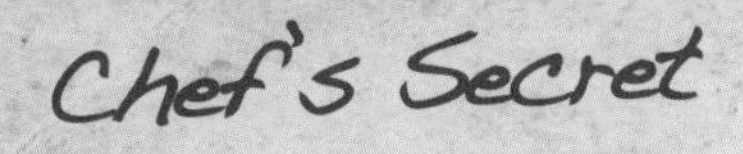

If you're from Sheffield then no further explanation will be required when we list Henderson's among the ingredients. For the benefit of those who are not so fortunate, it's a savoury sauce, a bit like Worcester Sauce - only better. This is a great supper dish, made all the more enjoyable by the satisfaction of having made your own bread.

Confit pork belly with black pudding, mashed potato and apple sauce

Ingredients

1kg pork belly
500g Duck or goose fat

FOR THE MASHED POTATO:

1kg desiree potatoes
100ml double cream
100ml semi-skimmed milk
150g butter
Few sprigs thyme
Few sprigs rosemary
Pinch of nutmeg
Pinch of white pepper

APPLE SAUCE:

2 Granny Smith apples
50g caster sugar
Juice 1 lemon
Seeds from half a vanilla pod
50ml water
50g butter

FOR THE BLACK PUDDING:

1 litre fresh pig's blood
1 onion, finely chopped
1 clove garlic
12 sage leaves, finely chopped
125g pork back fat, cut into 1cm cubes
75g sultanas
75g pearl barley, boiled until soft
75g porridge oats
Pinch white pepper

Method

To prepare the pork belly:

Warm the goose fat in a pan.
Place the pork belly in an ovenproof dish and cover with the fat.
Cover with tin foil and place in the oven at 120ºc for 3 hours 30 minutes-4 hours.
To test whether the pork is cooked, cut into the meat with a knife. If it cuts through with little resistance it is cooked.
Remove from the oven and allow to cool.
Take the pork from the fat and place between 2 flat baking trays.
Wrap the trays tightly in cling film and place a heavy weight on top, to compress for 24 hours.
Cut 4 square portions, remove the skin and fry fat side down until crisp.

To make the mashed potato:

Peel the potatoes, season with salt and boil until soft.
Infuse the cream, milk and butter, with the thyme and rosemary in a pan for 15 minutes.
Drain the potatoes in a colander and allow to steam for 2 minutes.
Mash the potatoes with a potato ricer.
Sieve the cream and milk mix and beat into the mashed potato until light and fluffy.
Season with salt, pepper and nutmeg.

For the apple sauce:

Peel and core the apple and chop into inch cubes.
Place all the ingredients except the butter in a pan and cook until soft.
Liquidise the apples and butter until smooth.
Pass through a fine sieve.

To make the black pudding:

Blend the blood with a stick blender until smooth.
Pass through a fine sieve.
Cook the onion, garlic and sage until soft and combine with the blood.
Add the remaining ingredients and cook over a low heat for 10-15 minutes.
Place the mix in a terrine mould lined with baking parchment and bake in a bain marie at 120ºc for 45 minutes.
Check the black pudding is cooked by placing a knife into the centre of the pudding. If clean, the pudding is cooked.
Remove from the oven and allow to cool.

Chef's Secret

We garnish this with crispy crackling - to make your crackling press the pig skin between two flat baking trays and bake until crispy.

Double eggs Benedict

Ingredients

8 rashers of home-cured bacon, grilled

8 poached eggs

200g spinach, wilted

FOR THE HOLLANDAISE SAUCE:

250g butter, melted and milk solids discarded

4 egg yolks

50ml white wine vinegar

Juice of half a lemon

Pinch of salt

TO MAKE THE MUFFINS:

500g bread flour

100g butter

Half pint of milk

15g fresh yeast

15g sugar

15g salt

Chef's Secret

This makes the perfect hangover cure, if you don't fancy making it on a hangover then get yourself over to The Milestone and have it made for you!

Method

For the hollandaise:

Mix the yolks and vinegar in a metal bowl and then whisk in a bain-marie until light, fluffy and doubled in size. Slowly pour in the melted butter, whisking continuously until all is incorporated. Season with salt and lemon. Keep in a warm place until ready to serve.

To make the muffins:

Warm the milk to 37°c and then whisk in the yeast, sugar and butter.

Add the salt to the flour and then mix all the ingredients together. Knead for 10 minutes. Cover the dough with a damp cloth and leave in a warm place to prove until doubled in size.

Remove and knead again for 5 minutes.

Weigh the muffins into 70g portions. Roll between your hands into neat balls. Allow to prove until almost doubled in size and then flatten the balls slightly and bake at 180°c for 10-15 minutes.

To assemble:

Top the muffins with the spinach, followed by the bacon, poached eggs and finally the hollandaise.

Duck hot pot layered with sweet potatoes

Chef's Secret

This our twist on a traditional hot pot. Why not try your own? Maybe using mutton or rabbit.

Ingredients

TO COOK THE DUCK LEGS:

5 duck legs

250g duck or goose fat

FOR THE HOT POT:

Large handful of parsley, finely chopped

2 carrots

2 sticks of celery

1 leek (white part only)

100ml reduced veal stock

1 sweet potato

50g Parmesan

10g butter

Method

To cook the duck:

First, slowly melt the duck/goose fat.

Place the duck legs in an ovenproof dish and carefully pour over the melted fat.

Place in the oven at 130°c for 2-2 hours 30 minutes. The duck should be falling off the bone and tender.

Remove the duck legs from the fat and allow to drain. Save the duck fat to use again.

Pick all the meat off the legs and discard the skin and bones.

For the hot pot:

Finely chop the carrot, celery and leek and then sweat in a little butter until soft but without colour.

Add the shredded duck meat, chopped parsley and veal stock.

Peel the sweet potato and slice thinly as you would for a potato hotpot.

Blanch in boiling salted water for 30 seconds to soften slightly.

Place the duck mix in pie dishes and then top with the sweet potato. Sprinkle over the grated parmesan.

Bake at 170°c until hot and golden brown.

Fish pie with pipérade

Chef's Secret

The pipérade adds a slightly smokey sweet and sour flavour to the dish, that really lifts it to new heights.

Ingredients

FOR THE PIPÉRADE:

4 red peppers, peeled and finely sliced

1 onion, finely sliced

Half teaspoon smoked paprika

1 clove of garlic

10ml sherry vinegar

FOR THE FISH PIE:

400g mashed potato

50g grated parmesan

700g diced mixed fish (smoked haddock, salmon and whiting is a good mix)

FOR THE BECHAMEL SAUCE:

150g butter

150g flour

1 litre milk, warmed

Good pinch of saffron

Method

For the pipérade:

Place all the ingredients in a saucepan and cook down slowly until all the liquid is cooked out of the onions and peppers.

For the bechamel sauce:

Melt the butter in a large pan and gradually stir in the flour. Cook for a few minutes without colouring.

Remove from the heat and allow to cool slightly then add the saffron.

Stir in the warmed milk gradually, bringing to the boil each time.

Place the fish in the sauce and then cook for a further 5 minutes.

To assemble:

Place a tablespoon of the pipérade in the bottom of an ovenproof dish, then spoon in the fish mixture. Top with the mashed potato and the grated parmesan. Bake at 180ºc for 20 minutes until piping hot and browned.

Goat's cheese deep dish tart with mixed bean cassoulet

Ingredients

FOR THE PASTRY:

250g plain flour
125g butter, cubed
1 teaspoon salt
1 egg yolks
1-2 tablespoons water to bind

FOR THE TART FILLING:

Half pint milk
Half pint cream
5 egg yolks
150g goat's cheese
Small bunch of tarragon leaves, chopped
1 teaspoon salt

FOR THE MIXED BEAN CASSOULET:

1 tin of cooked mixed beans (we soak dried beans overnight and then cook them, but for convenience a tin of cooked beans is quite acceptable)
100ml white wine
1 small onion, finely diced
1 clove garlic, crushed to a fine purée
100ml double cream
Juice of half a lemon
Salt
Tarragon, finely chopped

Method

For the pastry:

Sieve the flour into a bowl and rub in the butter rub until the mixture resembles breadcrumbs.

Add the salt, egg yolk and a tablespoon of the water and mix together to a smooth dough. Use extra water if necessary. Allow to rest in the fridge for 45 minutes. Roll out into a large sheet about the thickness of a pound coin and line an 22cm tart case.

Place a circular sheet of parchment in the bottom of the tart case and then line with baking beans. Bake at 170°c for 20-30 minutes. Remove the baking beans and bake the tart case for a further 5 minutes.

To make the filling:

Whisk the egg yolks and pour on the cream and milk. Break in the goat's cheese and warm the mixture to around 30°c over a bain marie. Add the chopped tarragon and salt.

Pour the filling into the tart case and bake at 130°c for 45 minutes to an hour. The tart should still have a slight custardy wobble.

For the mixed bean cassoulet:

Sweat the onions and garlic in a small amount of oil until cooked and translucent. Add the mixed beans and wine and reduce by two-thirds. Stir in the cream and reduce by half. Season the beans with lemon juice and salt. Finish with the chopped tarragon.

Rolled ham hock with seeds and deep fried duck egg

Ingredients

FOR THE HAM HOCK:

2 ham hocks

50g sunflower seeds, pumpkin seeds and sesame seeds

4 carrots

4 sticks celery

1 onion, peeled and quartered

FOR THE DUCK EGG:

4 duck eggs

1 egg, beaten

Flour for dusting

50g breadcrumbs

Method

To cook the ham hock:

Cover the ham hock with cold water in a saucepan and add 2 of the carrots (roughly chopped) with 2 sticks of celery (roughly chopped) and the diced onion.

Bring to the boil and then turn down to a gentle simmer. Skim any white scum from the top of the pan and simmer for a further 3 hours or until the meat is falling from the bone.

Remove the ham hocks and allow to cool, reserve the ham stock for another recipe.

When cool enough to handle, remove the hock meat and discard the bones and skin.

Chop 2 carrots into ½cm cubes and sweat down in a small amount of vegetable oil until soft but not coloured.

Mix through the ham hock meat and the seeds and, whilst still warm, roll up in cling film into a fat sausage about 2 inches thick.

Leave to set in the fridge then slice into 4 even portions.

For the duck egg:

Place the duck eggs in a pan of boiling water and then boil for 6-7 minutes; place into iced water to stop the cooking process.

Peel the eggs and then roll in the flour, roll in the beaten egg then through the breadcrumbs.

Deep fry at 180ºc until golden.

To assemble:

Pan-fry the ham hocks on either side and then place in the oven to heat through at 180ºc for 8 minutes.

Mackerel cooked in a bag with aromatics

Ingredients

- 4 whole mackerel, gutted and cleaned
- 150g chorizo
- 1 pak choi
- 1 lemon
- 1 lime
- 1 teaspoon pink peppercorns
- 1 teaspoon coriander seeds
- 4 star anise
- 4 cardamom pods
- 100g butter
- 200ml white wine
- 1 teaspoon salt

You'll also need some parchment paper

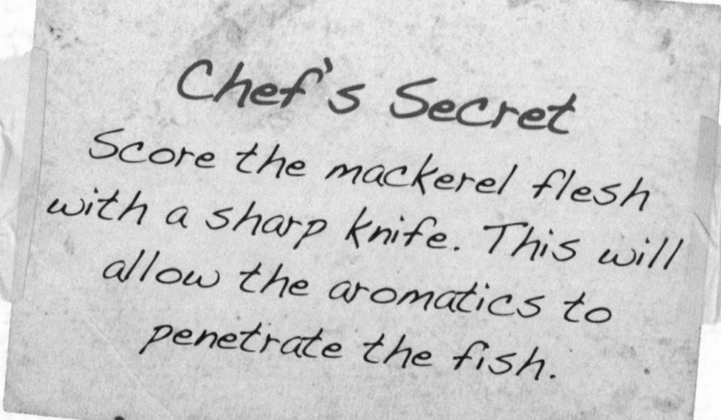

Chef's Secret

Score the mackerel flesh with a sharp knife. This will allow the aromatics to penetrate the fish.

Method

Lay each fish in the middle of large sheets of parchment paper.

Place all the remaining ingredients except the wine inside and around the fish. Fold the paper over it once, so that you have a rectangular shape with 3 open sides. Fold each of the edges in turn several times over (the effect is rather like a concertina) to seal them and keep everything enclosed in the parcel. Before folding the last of the open edges, pour in the wine and then tuck the parchment under the fish.

Bake at 180°c for 15-20 minutes.

The Milestone ploughman's

This is a ploughman's with a difference – one where you make everything except the cheese (though don't let us stop you if the urge takes you!) It's a variation on the traditional hot water crust pastry pork pie. Fabulous served with our pickled balsamic onions.

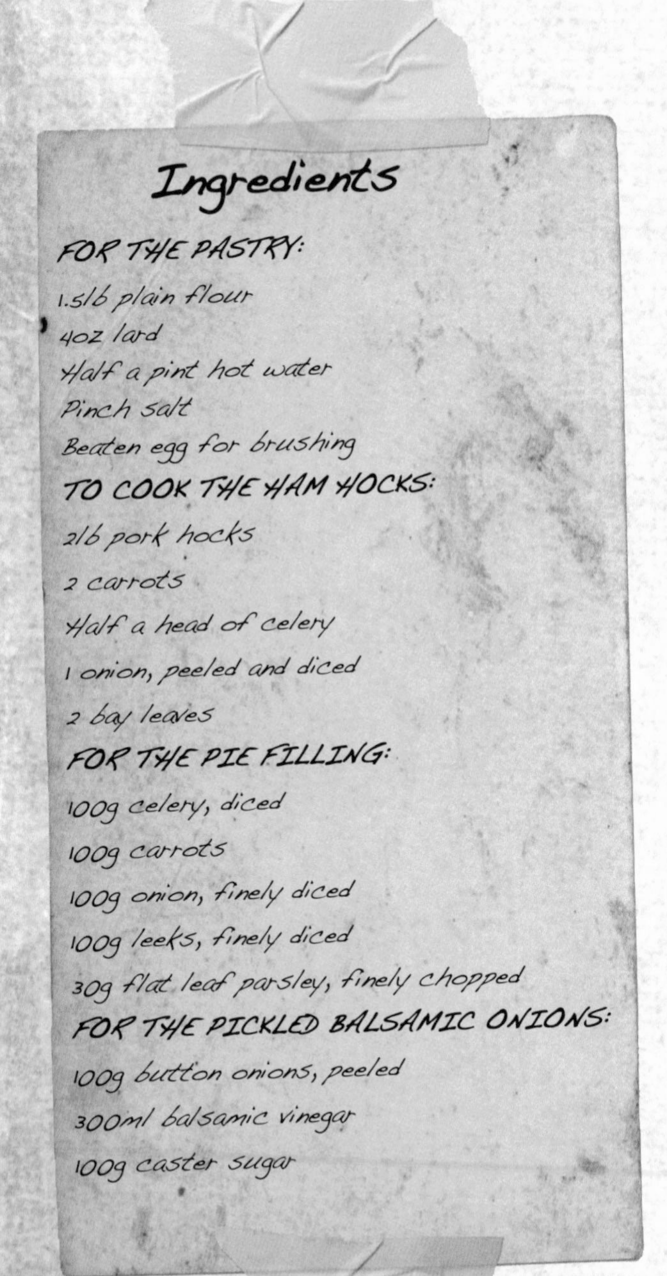

Ingredients

FOR THE PASTRY:

1.5lb plain flour

4oz lard

Half a pint hot water

Pinch salt

Beaten egg for brushing

TO COOK THE HAM HOCKS:

2lb pork hocks

2 carrots

Half a head of celery

1 onion, peeled and diced

2 bay leaves

FOR THE PIE FILLING:

100g celery, diced

100g carrots

100g onion, finely diced

100g leeks, finely diced

30g flat leaf parsley, finely chopped

FOR THE PICKLED BALSAMIC ONIONS:

100g button onions, peeled

300ml balsamic vinegar

100g caster sugar

Method

For the pastry:

Bring the water to the boil and add the lard and allow to dissolve.

Using a food processor, blend together all the remaining ingredients and mix to a dough.

For the ham hocks:

Place the first 5 ingredients in a large pan and cover with cold water.

Bring to the boil. Skim off any scum and fat that rises to the top of the pan. Simmer the hocks for 3 hours until tender.

Remove the hocks from the cooking liquor. Flake off all the meat when they are cool enough to handle and discard the vegetables.

Pass the cooking liquor through a sieve and then reduce by half.

For the pie filling:

Sweat the vegetables in a teaspoon of oil until cooked but without colour and then mix with the hock meat and the parsley.

To assemble:

Roll out the pastry to the thickness of a pound coin and place in a terrine mould.

Add the filling and then place another layer of pastry on top to seal.

Bake at 160ºc for 1 hour 30 minutes then place on a rack and allow to cool.

Once properly cool, make a small hole in the top of the pastry and pour in the cooking liquour. Allow it to set in the fridge and then slice.

To make the pickled balsamic onions:

Place the onions, vinegar and sugar in a pan and cook for 20 minutes until the onions are softened and the balsamic vinegar has thickened slightly.

Chef's Secret

Don't be afraid of putting too much cooking liquor in your pie, it really makes it extra special.

Mussels, leeks, cider, bacon and clotted cream

Ingredients

2kg mussels, cleaned and washed
200g streaky bacon, cut into thin strips
4 cloves garlic, crushed to a purée
2 leeks
100g clotted cream
Half pint apple cider
Handful parsley, finely chopped

Method

Finely shred the leeks and then sweat down in a little oil in a deep pan with the garlic and bacon then cook until soft.

Turn up the heat and add the mussels.

Place a lid on top of the pan and steam for 2-3 minutes until the mussels open.

Add the clotted cream last and stir through.

Finish with the chopped parsley.

Chef's Secret

This is a West Country take on the classic French dish, moules marinière – try your own version with a local beer

Nettle gnocchi, globe artichoke, roast garlic purée, cep cream and braised baby gem lettuce

Ingredients

FOR THE NETTLE GNOCCHI:

600g floury potatoes, such as King Edwards or Estima, peeled

150g nettle leaves

2 free-range egg yolks

120g plain flour

FOR THE ARTICHOKES:

4 artichokes

Half bottle of white wine

Few sprigs of thyme

400ml water

1 teaspoon salt

100ml olive oil

2 lemons

Handful of parsley stalks

ROAST GARLIC PURÉE:

4 heads of garlic

50g butter

CEP CREAM:

125ml white wine

125ml vegetable stock

125ml double cream

10g dried ceps

Juice 1 lemon

Method

For the nettle gnocchi:

Roast the potatoes in their skins until soft. Scoop out the flesh and discard the skins. Mash the potatoes or pass through a sieve.

Blanch the nettle leaves for 20 seconds in boiling salted water and then refresh in iced water. Drain and then squeeze out any excess moisture. Chop finely or place in a food processor.

Sieve the flour into the potatoes and then add the yolks and nettle mix together. Roll out into inch wide sausages, cut out at half inch intervals.

Blanch in boiling water until the gnocchi floats, then refresh in iced water. Once cold, remove from the water.

For the artichokes:

To prepare the artichokes, first cut off the stalks from the base. Carefully snap or pull off enough layers of the tough, green outer leaves until you reach the ones that are mostly yellow and therefore more tender. Cut the tips off these, then peel the tough green outside of the base of the artichoke, using a potato peeler or sharp knife, until you see yellow. With a teaspoon, scrape out all the furry material inside the artichoke. Place all the ingredients in a pan and bring to the boil. Simmer for 2 minutes and then allow the artichokes to cool in the liquor.

Roast the garlic in the skins at 140ºc for 45 minutes. Squeeze the garlic from the skins and the blend to a smooth purée with the butter in a liquidiser. Pass through a fine sieve to ensure it is completely smooth.

For the cep cream:

Place the ceps and white wine in a pan and then reduce by half. Add the vegetable stock and then reduce by half again. Add the double cream and then reduce again by half. Season with salt and the lemon juice.

To assemble:

Shred 2 baby gem lettuces. Pan-fry the gnocchi and the artichokes to colour slightly. Add the lettuce and a splash of the cream. Allow the lettuce to wilt down. Place the cep cream in the bottom of a bowl and then add the gnocchi and artichoke mix on top.

Spread a small spoonful of the garlic purée on the side of the plate and serve.

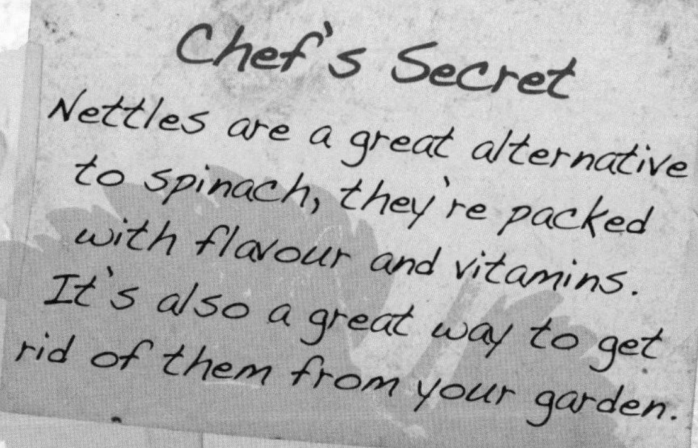
Chef's Secret
Nettles are a great alternative
to spinach, they're packed
with flavour and vitamins.
It's also a great way to get
rid of them from your garden.

Beef Bourguignon – slow cooked ox cheek, herb mashed potato and Bourguignon jus

Ingredients

4 ox cheeks
2 carrots, chopped
3 sticks celery, chopped
4 cloves garlic, crushed
Half bottle red wine
1 onion, peeled and quartered

(1 quantity of mash from the belly pork and black pudding dish on page 86)
1 handful of chopped parsley to add to the mash

FOR THE BOURGUIGNON

100g home cured bacon or pancetta, cut into 1 cm cubes
100g silverskin onions, peeled
Handful parsley, chopped
Ox cheek stock
1 large glass red wine

Method

To make the ox cheek:

Trim the fat from the ox cheek.

Heat the oil in a heavy-based frying pan and colour the ox cheeks on each side.

Remove and place in an ovenproof dish.

Colour the vegetables in the same pan and deglaze with the wine.

Reduce by two thirds and pour over the cheeks.

Cover with cold water and braise at 120°c for 8 hours.

Once tender, remove the cheeks.

Strain and reduce the stock.

For the Bourguignon sauce:

Colour the bacon in a saucepan.

Add the onions and wine and reduce.

Combine with the stock and simmer for 30 minutes.

Place a scoop of the mashed potato in a bowl and top with the braised beef cheek then pour over the Bourguignon sauce.

Chef's Secret
Beef cheeks need plenty of slow cooking but they are probably the most flavoursome cut of beef if treated with respect.

Boned and rolled pig's head with mashed potato and caper jus

Ingredients

FOR THE PIG'S HEAD:

1 pig's head (this is more than enough so use the extra for another dish)

2 carrots, peeled and chopped

4 sticks celery, peeled and chopped

1 star anise

1 onion, peeled and chopped

1 leek, (white only)

Half bottle of white wine

2 cloves garlic

Water to cover

TO SERVE:

12 cherry tomatoes, roasted

16 caperberries

Mashed potato (page 86)

Reduced veal stock (page 158)

Method

For the pig's head:

To bone out the pig's head, run a boning knife from the top of the skull following the bone round one side. Be careful to keep the knife scraping the bone so you don't break the skin. Ensure all the flesh is removed from the cheeks. Repeat on the other side of the head.

Remove the ears from the head and then remove any hairs either with a razor or blowtorch.

Butterfly the cheek meat and then place half a tongue in each half of head.

Season with salt and then roll up into a sausage shape with the skin on the outside protecting all the meat.

Roll up tightly in cling film to hold the shape. Place the remaining ingredients in an ovenproof dish and then cover with water. Braise at 140°c for 4-5 hours until tender. Take the pig's head out of the cooking liquor and allow to cool slightly.

When cool enough to handle, remove the cling film and then roll again tightly in more cling film to a neat cylinder. Use enough cling film to make it watertight and then place in iced water to cool.

To assemble:

Slice the pigs head into 4 portions and then pan-fry on each side to crisp up. Place in the oven at 170°c until hot.

Sit on top of the mashed potato and top with the tomato, caperberries and reduced veal stock.

Chef's Secret
You may find pig's head difficult to obtain in the supermarket - if you ask your butcher in advance it won't be a problem to get hold of.

Salt mackerel and sesame seed pasty with tomato marmalade and sautéed new potatoes

Ingredients

FOR THE SALT MACKEREL:

600g mackerel fillets, skin off and pinboned

250g Maldon sea salt

125g caster sugar

FOR THE FILLING:

50g each of leek, carrots, onions and celery, all peeled and diced into small cubes

1 tablespoon sesame oil

FOR THE PASTRY:

500g plain flour

250g unsalted butter

1 egg yolk

1 tablespoon water to bind

1 teaspoon salt

FOR THE TOMATO MARMALADE:

2 tins chopped tomatoes

100ml white wine vinegar

1 red chilli, finely chopped and seeds discarded

1 teaspoon paprika

100g caster sugar

Half onion, finely chopped

Method

For the filling:

Mix the salt and sugar together and then rub all over the mackerel fillets. Place on a tray and cover with cling film, then put in the fridge for three hours.

Wash the fillets in cold water and pat dry with kitchen roll. Cut into 2cm cubes.

Meanwhile, sweat the vegetables in a saucepan with the sesame oil until soft but without colouring. Allow to cool and then mix with the mackerel.

To make the pastry:

Mix the flour, salt and butter together until it resembles fine breadcrumbs.

Add the egg yolk and water. Mix together into a smooth dough. Be careful not to overwork the mix.

Wrap in cling film and allow to rest in the fridge for 1 hour.

To assemble the pasties:

Roll out the pastry to the thickness of a pound coin and then cut out an oval shape. Place some of the mackerel filling in the middle of the pastry then fold into the middle, sealing the pasty with a light layer of egg yolk. Crimp the pastry at the seam and then brush with beaten egg. Sprinkle with sesame seeds and allow to rest in the fridge for 30 minutes.

Bake at 180°c for 15-20 minutes.

To make the tomato marmalade:

Place the onion in a saucepan with a teaspoon of oil and sweat until soft but not coloured. Add the remaining ingredients then cook down till reduced by half (the marmalade should have a nice gloss and a sweet and sour taste).

To assemble:

Boil some new potatoes in salted water then pan-fry them in a little oil until golden. Mix with two tablespoons of the tomato marmalade. Finally, place a handful of spinach over the hot dish and allow it to wilt.

Stuffed pig's trotters

Ingredients

4 pigs trotters (ask your butcher for the large ones from the back legs)
200g pork mince
600g ham hock, cooked in the same way as for the ham and eggs on page 96
10g sage
1 egg yolk

FOR THE COOKING LIQUOR:
3 carrots
2 sticks of celery
1 bulb of garlic, chopped in half
1 onion, peeled and quartered
4 pints water

TO FINISH:
50g butter
50g honey

Method

For the liquor:

Place all the ingredients for the cooking liquor in a pan and bring to the boil. Turn down the heat and simmer for 30 minutes.

Prepare the trotters:

Bone the trotters out by using a sharp knife to cut just under the skin, running along the bone and peeling the skin back. Work carefully to ensure the skin is not punctured.

Remove the bone by cutting through at the knuckle. You will be left with what resembles a sock of skin.

Finely chop the sage and mix the with the pork mince, hock and egg yolk. Season with salt. Stuff the trotter skin, wrap in cling film to hold the shape and poach for 45 minutes in the cooking liquor.

Remove the trotters from the pan and place into a non-stick frying pan with the butter and honey and glaze before serving.

Serve with seasonal greens and roasted root vegetables.

Pan-fried plaice fillet with lemon pith purée, roast crayfish tails, muscat grapes, crayfish & elderflower velouté

Ingredients

1 fillet of plaice (about 6oz)
16 live crayfish
16 seedless white grapes
2 lemons
1 bulb of fennel
2 sticks of celery
Half a leek, white only
1 star anise
50ml Noilly Prat
1 small glass white wine
10 elderflower heads or dried elderflower
1 teaspoon tomato purée
A few pea shoots

TO MAKE THE LEMON PITH PURÉE:

2 lemons
75g sugar
30g butter

Method

To make the shellfish bisque:

To dispatch the crayfish, plunge into boiling salted water. Boil for 3 minutes, then refresh in iced water to stop the cooking process.

Peel the tails from the crayfish as you would a prawn and then reserve the shells and head for the sauce.

Clean the shells and heads of the crayfish and then roast at 180ºc for 15 minutes.

Finely chop the fennel, celery and leek and sweat down with a small amount of oil until softened.

Pour in the wine and Noilly Prat and reduce until there is barely any liquid left.

Add the tomato purée and cook for 2 minutes on a low heat.

Cover the crayfish shells with the water, star anise and lemon zest. Simmer for 30 minutes.

Add the elderflowers and place in a food processor. Blend until a fine sauce.

Pass the sauce through a fine strainer then reduce until thickened.

Season with salt and a squeeze of lemon juice.

To make the lemon pith purée:

Zest the lemons and set aside for the bisque. Squeeze them and save the juice.

Place the pith in a pan and cover with water. Bring to the boil and then refresh in cold water. Repeat twice more (this helps remove the bitterness from the pith).

Place the pith, sugar and butter in a liquidiser and blend to a fine purée. Pass through a fine sieve and season with salt.

To assemble:

Pan-fry the plaice in a non-stick pan until golden. Pour the lemon juice into the pan along with the butter, then the cooked crayfish and the grapes to heat through and glaze the plaice with the butter.

Spread the pith purée on a plate followed by the plaice, grapes and crayfish. Finish with the bisque and pea shoots.

Chef's Secret

The freshwater Signal crayfish are a pest and are killing our native crayfish. Do your part for the environment and eat more of them!

Poussin, chateau potatoes, chicken velouté, sage crisps

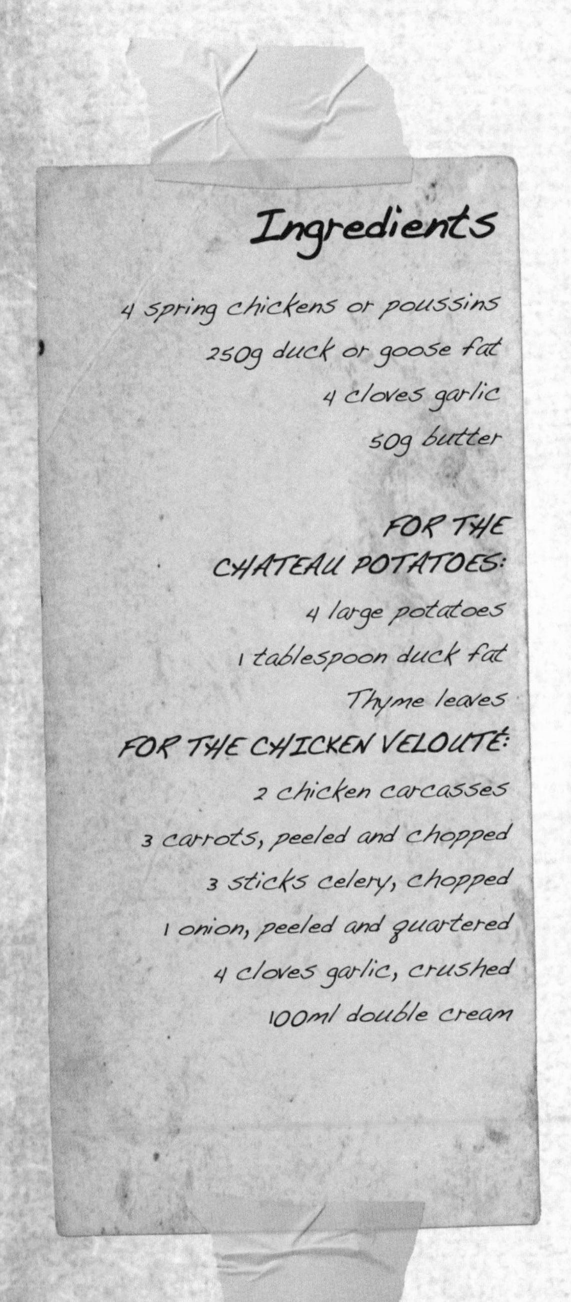

Method

To prepare the chicken:

Remove the legs from the carcass and then trim through to free the crown.

Place the legs in a ovenproof dish. Coat with the duck fat, cover with tin foil and then place in a pre-heated oven at 120ºc for 1 hour 30 minutes until tender.

Remove the legs from the confit fat and allow to cool.

To roast the crown, place in a frying pan skin side down until golden and crisp. Turn over and colour. Add a few sprigs of thyme, a clove of garlic and the butter to the pan. Top up with water until the chicken is half submerged. Place in the oven at 180ºc for 10 minutes.

For the chateau potatoes:

Peel the potatoes with a paring knife and turn into barrel shapes. Place the duck fat in a pan and colour the potatoes. Transfer to a roasting tin, sprinkle on the thyme leaves and roast at 170ºc for 35 minutes until soft and golden.

Chicken velouté:

Place all the ingredients except the cream into a pan and cover with cold water. Bring to the boil and then turn down to a simmer. Skim off the white scum and cook out for 1 hour 30 minutes on a gentle simmer.

Pass the stock through a fine strainer and then skim any remaining fat or scum away.

Add the cream and reduce until a glossy sauce consistency.

To assemble:

Place the legs skin side down in a hot pan until crisp, then top with the chicken crown.

Place the chateau potatoes on the plate and then finish with the sauce. Add a few deep fried sage leaves for a garnish if the mood takes you.

Chef's Secret
Here's a great way of cooking chicken. The water in the pan will keep the chicken moist whilst still crisping the skin.

Rabbit loin, carrot purée, sauted lettuce with rabbit leg, courgette and pigs tail cannelloni and a rabbit jus

Ingredients

2 wild rabbits
4 pig's tails
2 carrots, chopped
2 sticks celery, chopped
1 onion, peeled and quartered
Few sprigs thyme
Few sprigs rosemary

FOR THE CANNELLONI:

Braised rabbit meat and pig's tail
Handful parsley, finely chopped
2 courgettes, thinly sliced
2 teaspoons rabbit stock, reduced

FOR THE CARROT PURÉE:

2 carrots, peeled and finely chopped
20ml honey
30g butter

FOR THE BRAISED BABY GEM LETTUCE:

50g butter
100ml chicken stock
2 baby gem lettuce

Method

To prepare the rabbit:

Remove the legs from the rabbit and set aside for braising.
Cut off the loin and set aside.
Place the carrots, onion and celery, rabbit legs, pig's tail and rabbit carcass into an ovenproof dish and cover with cold water.
Create a tin foil lid and cook in a pre-heated oven at 140ºc for 2 hours.
Remove the meat from the liquid and allow to cool.
Cut the meat off the pig's tail and rabbit legs, discarding any bones.
Strain the cooking liquid, skim off excess fat and reduce.

To make the cannelloni:

Blanch the courgette strips in boiling water for 5 seconds.
Refresh in iced water.
Remove from the water and pat dry.
Mix the remaining ingredients together and roll into a thin cylinder.
Overlap the courgette strips on a sheet of cling film.
Lay the meat on the courgette and roll into a cannelloni.
Tie each end of the cling film, ensuring it is watertight.

For the carrot purée:

Place carrots and honey in a saucepan and cover with water.
Bring to the boil and cook until soft.
Liquidise with a tablespoon of cooking liquid and blend into a fine purée.
Add the butter and mix to emulsify.
Pass through a fine sieve and season with salt.

For the baby gem lettuce:

Rub the lettuce with butter and set in the fridge.
Place into a hot frying pan to colour.
Add the stock and remaining butter and cook over a high heat.
Baste with butter and stock and season with a pinch of salt.

To assemble:

Pan-fry the rabbit loins.
Place the cannelloni in boiling water and heat through.
Spread a spoonful of purée on a plate.
Top with the cannelloni, rabbit loin and lettuce.
Drizzle the rabbit stock over the dish.

Chef's Secret
This is the gardener's revenge, serving the rabbit with the lettuce and the carrot.

Rack of lamb, wild garlic purée, wilted spinach with a trompette jus

Ingredients

4 x four bone best end of lamb, French trimmed

TO MAKE THE VEAL STOCK/TROMPETTE JUS:

4kg veal bones
2 calves feet
4 litres water
400g carrots, chopped
200g onions, chopped
100g celery, chopped
1kg tomatoes
200g trompette mushrooms
Bouquet garni
4 cloves garlic

200g spinach, wilted

FOR THE PURÉE:

300g wild garlic leaves

Method

For the wild garlic purée:

Bring a large pan of water to the boil. Blanch the wild garlic for 10 seconds then transfer to a liquidiser. Blend with a small amount of the blanching water until a fine smooth purée.

For the stock:

In a very large pan, brown the bones and feet in a little oil. Place the bones in a stock pot, cover with cold water and bring to simmer.

Roast the onions, carrots and celery with fat from bones. Drain off fat and add vegetables to stock and deglaze the tray. Add tomatoes, mushrooms and garlic and simmer for 10 hours. Skim frequently.

Strain and reduce until the sauce thickens and has an intense flavour. Finally, add the trompette mushrooms.

For the lamb rack:

Heat oil in a large frying pan. Cook the lamb to colour all over then turn so that the fatty skin side is downwards. Cook for a few minutes, then place the lamb in the oven at 180ºc for 8-16 minutes depending on how pink you want your lamb. Wilt a few spinach leaves in a pan with a small amount of butter and season with salt.

To assemble:

Spread a line of the purée on a plate. Spoon on the spinach. Cut the lamb rack in half, place on the plate and pour over a small amount of the jus and trompette mushrooms.

Chef's Secret

Wild garlic grows in wooded conditions next to waterways from March to May.

You'll smell the heavy garlic aroma before you spot the plant.

Don't pick wild plants to eat unless you're an experienced forager.

Rump beef and chestnuts, braised short ribs, tea-infused fondant potato with beef jus

Ingredients

4 x 6oz rump steaks, trimmed of any sinew and fat
4 x 6oz short rib pieces
4 large potatoes
3 Earl Grey teabags
200ml beef stock
50g butter
2 carrots
2 celery sticks
1 onion, peeled and quartered
Few sprigs thyme and rosemary
Half bottle red wine
100g pre-cooked chestnuts

Method

For the potatoes:
Using a ring cutter, cut out cylinders of potato, trim off any skin and neaten the shape. Pan-fry each of the fondants in a little vegetable oil on each side until golden. Add the stock, butter and tea bags and then place in a pre-heated oven at 170ºc for 45 minutes until soft.

For the braised shortribs:
Pan-fry the ribs on each side to get a good colour. Remove from the pan and replace with the onion, celery and carrot. Cook until brown. Remove from the pan and place in an ovenproof container with the ribs. Add the wine to the pan. Deglaze and then reduce by two-thirds. Pour over the ribs, add the thyme and rosemary and top up with cold water. Cover with foil and cook at 150ºc for 4 hours until tender.

Remove from the cooking liquor and strain, skim off any fat and reduce down to an intensely-flavoured sauce.

To assemble:
Pan-fry the rump steaks until rare and allow to rest. Cook the chestnuts in the same pan as the meat and then arrange the rump, shortrib, fondant potato and chestnuts on a plate. Finish with the sauce.

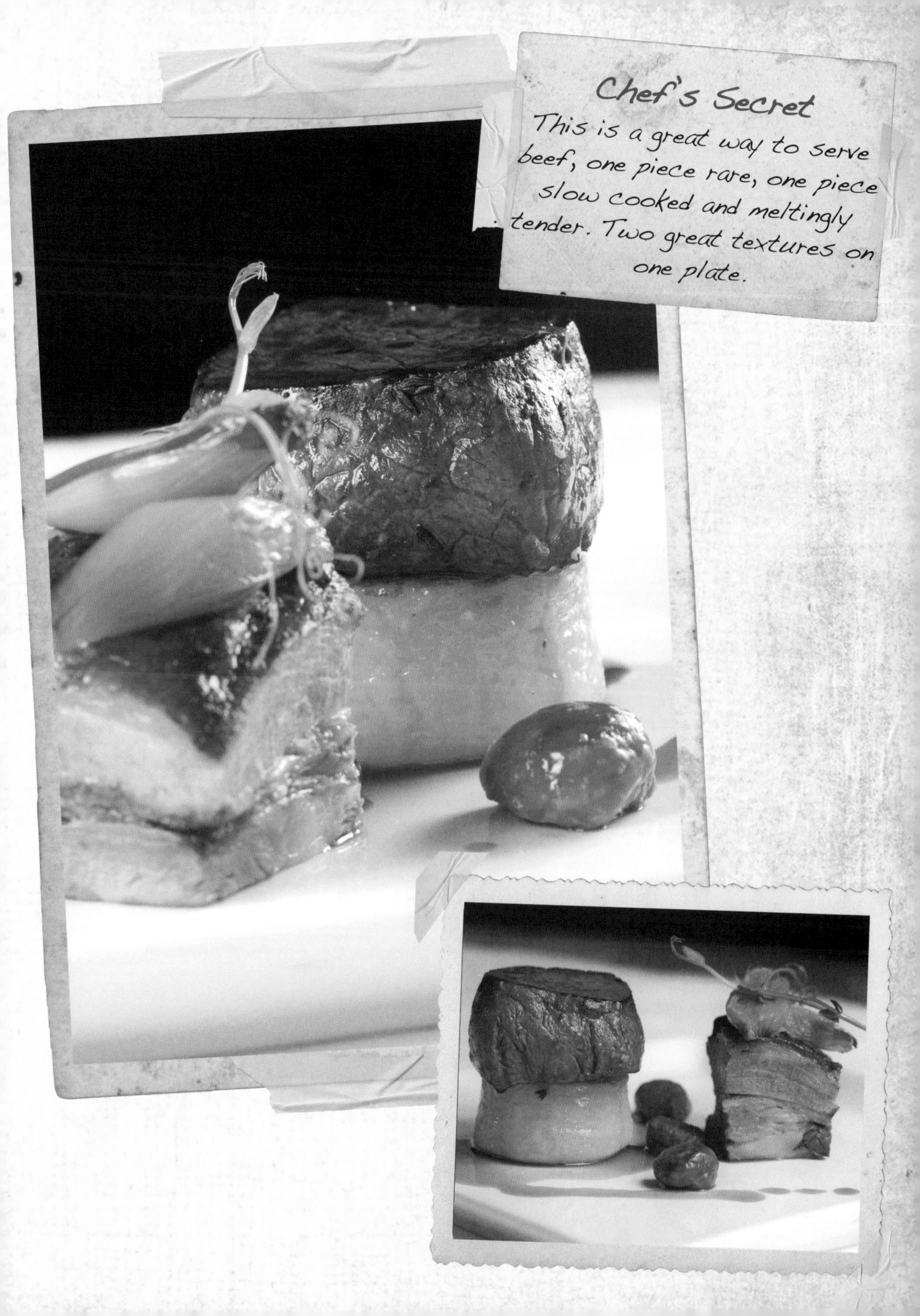
Chef's Secret
This is a great way to serve beef, one piece rare, one piece slow cooked and meltingly tender. Two great textures on one plate.

Rump beef, sweetbread, oxtail and tongue cottage pie watercress purée

Ingredients

4 x 170g beef rump portions, trimmed

100ml veal jus, reduced

1 ox tongue

2 carrots

2 sticks celery

3 cloves garlic

1 onion, peeled and quartered

Thyme leaves

See Watercress purée on page 134

To cook the oxtail – see turbot poached in merlot recipe on page 130

FOR THE COTTAGE PIE:

1 carrot, peeled and chopped into half centimetre cubes

1 stick celery, peeled and chopped into half centimetre cubes

50g peas

200g mashed potato

FOR THE SWEETBREADS:

200g sweetbreads

2 carrots

2 sticks celery

3 cloves garlic

1 onion, peeled and quartered

500ml water

Method

To make the cottage pie filling:

Place the ox tongue in a saucepan, cover with water and bring to the boil.

Run cold water onto the pan to refresh.

Cover in cold water and add the remaining ingredients.

Bring to the boil and simmer for 2 hours and 30 minutes.

When cool, peel the skin off the tongue and dice into 1cm cubes.

Mix the tongue, tail, sweetbreads, vegetables and oxtail cooking juices in a saucepan and cook until tender.

Place the mix into individual cottage pie dishes and top with the mashed potato.

Cook at 180ºc for 15 minutes or until glazed.

To make the sweetbreads:

Place the ingredients in a saucepan and bring to the boil.

Simmer for 10 minutes.

Add the sweetbreads and poach for 15 minutes.

Remove the liquid and cool in iced water.

Peel the outer membrane from the sweetbreads and slice into 1cm cubes.

To assemble:

Pan-fry the steak with a little butter and thyme leaves until rare.

Warm the watercress purée and spread onto a plate.

Add the steak and cottage pie.

Drizzle over the veal stock.

Chef's Secret
Cottage pie with a Milestone twist, using offal rather than traditional minced meat.

Pan-fried salmon with roasted radish, nettle gnocchi, crab faggots and lemon balm emulsion

Ingredients

4 x 170g salmon portions

FOR THE CRAB FAGGOT:

120g brown crab meat

120g white crab meat

4 iceberg lettuce leaves

1 red chilli, de-seeded and finely chopped

Small handful fresh coriander

1 shallot, finely diced

1 tablespoon crème frâiche

1 lime, juiced and zested

FOR THE LEMON BALM EMULSION:

Large handful lemon balm, finely chopped

1 egg yolk

100ml vegetable oil

20ml water

10ml white wine vinegar

Half teaspoon lethicin powder

12 breakfast radishes

Nettle gnocchi see the recipe on page 104

Method

Lemon balm emulsion:

Whisk the white wine vinegar, egg yolk and lethecin until light, pale and doubled in size.

Slowly pour in the oil and whisk constantly.

Add the water slowly whilst whisking.

Season with salt and add finely chopped lemon balm.

To make the crab faggot:

Mix the crab meat, crème frâiche, lime juice and zest, shallot, chilli and coriander.

Season with salt and place in refrigerator until ready to use.

Remove the tough stalk from the middle of the lettuce and blanch the leaves in boiling salted water for 8 seconds until wilted.

Squeeze excess water from the leaves.

Place a ball of the crab mix in the centre of each leaf.

Roll into a tight ball and wrap in cling film, ensuring it is watertight.

For the nettle gnocchi:

See recipe on page 104.

To assemble:

Pan-fry the salmon, skin side down, until crisp and golden.

Turn on each side to seal.

Place in the oven at 180ºc for 5 minutes.

Cut the radish in half and pan-fry with the gnocchi.

Place the crab in a pan of boiling water to heat.

Dress the plate with the lemon balm emulsion.

Lay the radish and gnocchi on top and place the crab faggot to one side.

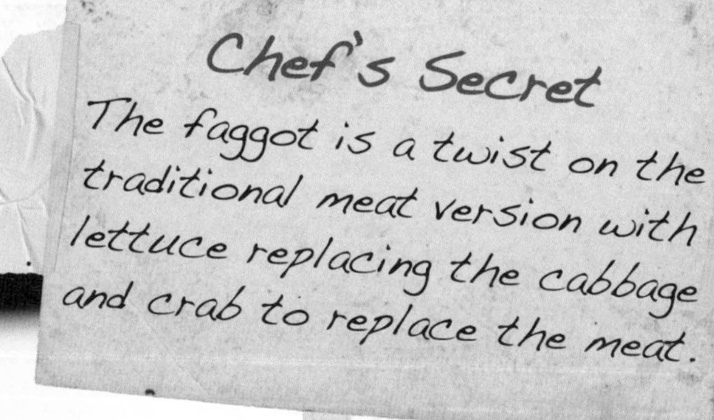
Chef's Secret
The faggot is a twist on the traditional meat version with lettuce replacing the cabbage and crab to replace the meat.

Salmon with a cardamom crust, sautéed new potatoes, cucumber and caper dressing

Ingredients

4 x 6oz salmon portions, skinless
300g boiled new potatoes, cooked and cooled
1 cucumber, halved and de-seeded

CAPER DRESSING:

30g capers drained from their brine
1 small bunch parsley, chopped
50ml olive oil
20ml white wine vinegar

CARDAMOM CRUST:

3 cardamoms pods, crushed
1 large handful parsley, finely chopped
1 large handful of coriander, finely chopped
50g breadcrumbs
1 egg yolk

Method

Caper dressing:

Fry the capers with a teaspoon of oil in a non-stick frying pan until they are nice and crisp. Remove from the pan and place in a mixing bowl with the vinegar and oil. Whisk to emulsify. Add the finely chopped parsley and season to taste with salt

For the cardamom crust:

In a dry frying pan toast the cardamom pods to release the essential oils and then crush to a paste in a pestle and mortar. Place the remaining ingredients in a food processor, including the cardamom and pulse to reduce to a fine paste. Place a layer of the crust about the thickness of a pound coin on top of the salmon and then allow to rest in the fridge for 30 minutes.

To finish:

Place the salmon in the oven at 180ºc for 10-12 minutes. Heat a non-stick pan with a splash of vegetable oil and saute the new potatoes and cucumber. Place the cucumber and potatoes in the centre of the dish. Rest the salmon on top and dress the dish with the caper dressing.

Turbot poached in red wine with oxtail, spinach and baby onions

Ingredients

200g spinach, wilted

FOR THE OXTAIL:

1kg oxtail

2 carrots

2 sticks celery

1 onion, peeled and quartered

4 cloves garlic

Few sprigs thyme

Few sprigs rosemary

Half bottle red wine

Water to cover

FOR THE TURBOT:

4x 170g turbot portions,
skin left on

Half bottle merlot
or other full bodied red wine

FOR THE RED WINE ONIONS:

6 button onions

250ml red wine

50g caster sugar

Method

To make the turbot:

Bring the red wine to the boil in a saucepan and add the turbot.

Reduce to a simmer until cooked. The fish will flake easily if cooked.

To make the oxtail:

Pan-fry the oxtail until golden and place in an ovenproof dish.

In the frying pan, cook the vegetables until coloured.

Add the red wine and reduce by two thirds.

Add the vegetables and red wine to the ovenproof dish and cover with water.

Create a tin foil lid and cook in the oven at 140ºc for 5 hours until tender.

Remove the oxtail and allow to cool.

Strip the meat from the bones, discarding all bones.

Transfer the cooking liquid to a sauce pan and reduce to a thick sauce consistency.

To make the sauce:

Peel the onions, leaving the roots intact to prevent it breaking apart.

Place the red wine, sugar and onions in a saucepan and simmer for 1 hour until soft.

To assemble:

Place the spinach in the bottom of a bowl.

Lay the turbot and oxtail on top of the spinach.

Scatter pieces of onion on each plate and drizzle with the sauce.

Chef's Secret
The turbot is a magnificent
fish and can take on the bold
flavours of red wine and
oxtail and still hold its own.

Venison heart meatballs in a tomato sauce with watercress pilaf rice

Ingredients

FOR THE MEATBALLS:

500g venison heart mince

300g venison mince

1 teaspoon piri piri flakes

1 egg yolk to bind

Flour to dust with

Salt

FOR THE TOMATO SAUCE:

1 onion finely diced

1 teaspoon piri piri flakes

2 cloves garlic

175ml red wine

4 tins chopped tomatoes

1 teaspoon thyme leaves

20ml balsamic vinegar

20g caster sugar

FOR THE RICE PILAF:

220g long grain rice

500ml vegetable stock

FOR THE WATERCRESS PURÉE:

200g watercress washed

Method

For the meatballs:

Mix all the ingredients together except the flour and then cook a small piece of the meatball mix. Taste the seasoning and adjust if required.

Roll into balls and coat with flour and then colour in a frying pan with a little oil.

Place in a roasting tray and then bake at 180°c for 20-30 minutes, depending on the size of the meatballs, check to see they are cooked through.

For the tomato sauce:

Finely dice the onion and garlic and then cook with the chilli flakes until soft but with no colour.

Add the red wine and reduce by two thirds.

Add the remaining ingredients and reduce further by a quarter.

Blend the sauce in a liquidiser and then pass through a sieve.

Add the meatballs and leave to marinate in the sauce, preferably overnight but an hour will suffice.

For the rice:

Place the rice and stock into an ovenproof dish and cover with cling film.

Cook at 170°c for 20-30 minutes until the rice is soft.

For the watercress purée:

Bring a large pan of water to the boil and then add the watercress for 10 seconds until wilted, remove and then purée in a liquidiser with a small amount of the cooking liquor until smooth.

To assemble:

Warm the meatballs in the sauce. Warm the rice with a teaspoon of water and add the watercress purée.

Place the rice on the bottom of the plate and top with the meatballs and sauce. Garnish with watercress.

Chef's Secret

You may find venison hearts difficult to obtain, why not substitute for lambs heart. This is a real thrifty dish but packed with flavour.

Sous vide venison loin, nettle and haunch wellington, watercress purée, beetroot fondant, braised baby gem lettuce and game gravy

Ingredients

FOR THE VENISON HAUNCH:

450g venison haunch
2 large carrots, chopped
1 large white onion, peeled and chopped
1 leek, chopped
2 garlic cloves, crushed
2 celery sticks, chopped
Small bunch thyme
100ml port
250ml merlot
150ml chicken stock
500ml venison stock

FOR THE PANCAKES:

100g plain flour
1 egg
1 egg yolk
Pinch salt
285ml milk
200g nettles, wilted and puréed
10g butter, melted

FOR THE PUFF PASTRY:

200g plain flour, plus extra for dusting
Pinch salt
200g butter, at room temperature
125ml ice cold water
1 egg yolk, for brushing

FOR THE WELLINGTON:

1 egg yolk, beaten with 2 tablespoons water

FOR THE VENISON LOIN:

1 450g venison loin
20g butter
4 thyme sprigs, each wrapped in cling film
Sunflower oil
Sea salt and freshly ground black pepper

FOR THE GRAVY:

100g butter
750g mushrooms, finely sliced
350g shallots, finely sliced
350g venison trim, diced
100ml sherry vinegar
700ml red wine
500ml veal stock
1 litre venison stock

FOR THE WATERCRESS PURÉE:

250g watercress
50g spinach
25g flat leaf parsley, picked
10g butter

FOR THE BEETROOT FONDANT:

4 large beetroot
150ml chicken stock
25g butter
Few thyme sprigs

FOR THE BABY GEMS:

2 baby gem lettuce, cut in half and outer leaves trimmed
50g butter
150ml vegetable stock

Chef's Secret

This recipe, though very complex is well worth the effort as it helped us win the title of 'Best British' in Gordon Ramsay's Best Restaurant competition.

Sous vide venison loin method

For the venison haunch:
Preheat the oven to 120ºc.
Trim the venison and cut into 2cm cubes.
Heat sunflower oil in a pan and fry the cubes to form a rich brown seal.
Remove the meat and add the carrot, onion, leek, garlic and celery.
Add the thyme to infuse the oil.
Remove the vegetables and pour in the port and wine to deglaze the pan.
Reduce by half and pour into an ovenproof dish with the remaining ingredients.
Cover with foil and braise in the oven for 8 hours.
Remove from oven and allow to cool then shred the meat with a fork.
Pass the braising liquid through a sieve and reduce to 100ml.
Mix the stock into the shredded meat and roll in cling film into a cylinder.
Allow to set in the refrigerator for 1-1 hour 30 minutes.
For the pancakes:
Whisk together the flour and add the egg yolk, milk and nettles. Fold in the butter.
Leave to rest for at least 30 minutes.
Heat the sunflower oil in a non-stick pan.
Pour the batter into the pan, to your desired thickness.
Cook on both sides until golden.
For the puff pastry:
Sift together the flour and the salt and rub in the butter. Stir in enough of the water to make a soft dough, wrap in cling film and chill for 20 minutes.
Put the butter between 2 pieces of greaseproof paper and flatten out with a rolling pin until it is a rectangle 10 x 7.5cm.
Roll out the dough to another rectangle that measures 12.5 x 25cm.
Take the butter out of the paper and put on the dough rectangle. Bring the corners of the dough together to make an envelope. Chill for 10 minutes.
Roll out the envelope on a floured surface to make a rectangle that is 3 times longer than it is wide. Fold one third into the middle and then the other third on top. Seal the edges lightly with a rolling pin and turn the pastry 90 degrees. Repeat and chill for 30 minutes.
Repeat this rolling and folding twice more and then chill for another 30 minutes and then do 2 more – the pastry will have been rolled and folded 6 times altogether.
Now roll out and use as required.
It is important that the pastry is well chilled otherwise the pastry will become greasy and tough when baked. Also the butter might come through the surface, if this happens, dab on a little flour.
To make the wellington:
Preheat the oven to 180ºc.
Roll the pastry to a 3mm thickness.
Cut into a square of 125mm x 125 mm.
Cut a pancake into a square of 125mm x 125mm.
Place the pancake atop the pastry.
Place the 80g of braised venison in the centre on top of the pancake.
Roll the edges together to make an individual portion.
Brush with the egg wash and sprinkle with sea salt.
Refrigerate for 15 minutes before baking for 15-20 minutes.
To make the venison loin:
Trim off any sinews from the venison loin.
Cut into 4 portions and place each in a vacuum pouch with 5g butter.
Place a cling film wrapped spring of thyme in each pouch and vacuum pack.
Place in a water bath set to 54ºc for 20-25 minutes.
Once cooked, remove from the pouch and pat dry.
Heat a drizzle of sunflower oil in a pan and colour the venison.
For the gravy:
Heat the butter in the pan, caramelise the shallots and mushrooms and strain.
Heat the remaining butter in another pan and caramelise the venison until golden. Deglaze the pans with the vinegar.
In a separate pan, reduce the wine by half.
Add the stock and remaining ingredients. Reduce to a sauce consistency and strain.
To make the watercress purée:
Wash the cress, spinach and parsley and drain well.
Blanch in a deep pan of boiling water for 10 seconds and drain.
Blend with a stick blender into a purée.
Add the butter to emulsify and season with salt.
Pass through a fine sieve into a metal bowl. This will help to chill the purée and prevent colour loss.
To make the beetroot fondant:
Peel the beetroot.
Using a 38mm ring cutter, cut each beetroot.
Trim the beetroot discs to 25mm high and neaten the edges.
Place in a hot frying pan to colour.
Lay in a shallow dish with the chicken stock, butter and thyme and bake in the oven at 180ºc for 20-30 minutes.
To make the baby gem lettuce:
Rub the lettuce with 20g butter and place in the refrigerator to set.
Colour the gem halves in a frying pan.
Add the stock and remaining butter and cook on a high heat, basting the lettuce.
Season with a pinch of salt.
To assemble:
Spread a small spoonful of the purée across the plate.
Place the loin, wellington and fondant alongside.
Rest the baby gem atop the fondant and spoon the gravy over the loin.

Chef's Secret
As you can see, puff pastry is a labour of love, good quality pre-made puff pastry is acceptable and easily available.

Yorkshire pudding, braised shin of beef and root vegetables

Ingredients

FOR THE SHIN OF BEEF:
1kg beef shin, cut into 4 pieces
100g flour
2 carrots, peeled and chopped
3 sticks celery, chopped
1 onion, peeled and quartered
Few sprigs thyme
Few sprigs rosemary
Half bottle red wine
5 cloves garlic

FOR THE YORKSHIRE PUDDING:
100g plain flour
3 eggs
200ml milk
Pinch of salt
5 ice cubes

ROOT VEGETABLES:
2 carrots
1 swede
4 parsnips
1 tablespoon honey
50g butter

Method

To make the beef shin:

In a heavy frying pan add the vegetable oil and gently fry to colour the beef.

Remove the beef from the pan and add the vegetables, fry these until slightly coloured also.

Add the red wine and reduce by two thirds.

Place all the ingredients in an ovenproof dish and cover with water.

Create a tin foil lid and braise at 140°c for 5 hours until tender.

Remove the meat from the liquid, strain the stock through a fine sieve and reduce, this will be used for the sauce.

For the Yorkshire pudding:

Mix together all the ingredients except the ice cubes.

Place the ice cubes in a fine sieve and pour the mixture through over the ice cubes.

Pour a small amount of oil in a large Yorkshire pudding tray in the oven at 200°c until smoking.

Fill with the Yorkshire pudding mix and cook for 25-30 minutes.

To roast the root vegetables:

Peel all the vegetables and chop into 3cm cubes.

Melt the butter in a frying pan, add the vegetables and colour.

Add honey and roast at 180°c for 20-25 minutes until soft.

To assemble:

Place the root vegetables inside the Yorkshire pudding.

Top with the beef shin and the reduced sauce.

Chef's Secret
Passing the Yorkie batter
through ice really
makes the puddings
rise that extra mile!

Baked apple stuffed with raisins, custard with rum and raisin ice cream

Ingredients

FOR THE BAKED APPLES:

4 Braeburn apples, cored

50g fresh bread crumbs

75g demerara sugar

30g raisins

75ml dark rum

FOR THE CUSTARD:

250ml milk

250ml double cream

50g caster sugar

1 vanilla pod

6 large egg yolks

For the ice cream see our basic recipe on page 160

Method

For the baked apples:

Soak the raisins in the rum with half the sugar for 24 hours. Press a small ball of breadcrumbs into one end of the cored apples to seal the hole. Combine the rum and remaining sugar and stuff the apples until full to the brim. Pour in any of the rum that the raisins have not soaked up.

Wrap the apples in tin foil and bake at 170ºc for 20-25 minutes until the apples are soft.

To make home-made custard:

Place the milk, vanilla and cream in a saucepan and bring to the boil. Whisk together the yolks and sugar until light and pale. Add the milk and cream mix and continue whisking. Simmer until the mixture thickens enough to coat the back of a wooden spoon. Do not allow to boil as this will make the custard scramble.

Bakewell tart with amaretto ice cream

Ingredients

FOR THE FRANGIPANE MIX:

160g diced unsalted butter, at room temperature
160g icing sugar
160g ground almonds
30g plain flour (sieved twice)
4 small or 3 large eggs (beaten)

FOR THE SWEET PASTRY:

1 lemon, zested
225g plain flour
75g sugar
150g diced well-chilled unsalted butter
3g salt (if using unsalted butter)
1 egg yolk
1 whole egg

150g raspberry jam

For the amaretto ice cream see our basic recipe on page 160

Method

Frangipane mix:

In a bowl, cream eggs and butter, adding one egg at a time to the butter. Once all eggs are incorporated add all remaining ingredients, stir to combine then chill.

Sweet pastry:

Place all dry ingredients in mixing bowl. Slowly incorporate butter using a rubbing-in method with the tips of your fingers until the mixture is a sandy consistency

Beat the eggs together and add, mix until a soft dough texture then refrigerate in the fridge for a minimum of 1 hour.

Roll pastry until thin. Place in tart cases then blind bake with baking beans on top of a layer of parchment for approximately 20 minutes on 180°c. Keep checking during baking. Remove from the oven. Leave in the cases to cool but remove the baking beans.

To assemble:

Spread a thin layer of raspberry jam onto the tart case

Fill the tart case two thirds full of your frangipane mixture and bake at 185°c until golden and firm.

Remove the tart from the case and leave to cool on a cooling rack.

Chilled peach and Champagne soup with strawberry pannacotta

Ingredients

FOR THE SOUP:

1kg slightly overripe peaches
200ml Champagne
300g caster sugar
Juice of half a lemon

FOR THE PANNACOTTA:

300ml double cream
300ml strawberry purée (made from 400g strawberries, 100g caster sugar, 50ml water cooked till soft then blended in a liquidiser and passed through a fine sieve)
50g caster sugar
4 sheets gelatine (soaked in cold water till soft)

Method

To make the soup:

Halve the peaches and stone them.

Place in an ovenproof dish and cover with tin foil then roast for 20 minutes at 180°c.

Meanwhile place the Champagne and lemon juice in a saucepan with the sugar and heat until dissolved.

Put the peaches and the Champagne mixture in a liquidiser and blend until really smooth. Pass the mixture through a fine sieve, using a ladle to push the mix through.

Taste and if necessary add more sugar – the actual amount will depend on how ripe the peaches are.

Chill the soup in the fridge until ready to serve.

For the panncotta:

Place the cream, strawberry purée and caster sugar in a saucepan and bring to the boil.

Take the gelatine out of the water and squeeze out any excess liquid then whisk into the cream and strawberry mix.

Once fully dissolved place into dariole moulds (metal moulds) and allow to set in the fridge.

To assemble:

Dip the dariole moulds into boiling water for 2 seconds to help the pannacotta turn out.

Place in a bowl and then half fill with the peach soup.

Garnish with fresh strawberry quarters and serve.

Chocolate and beetroot cake with cinder toffee

Ingredients

FOR THE CAKE:

250g dark chocolate (melted)
3 eggs
1kg demerara sugar
2 tablespoons black treacle
2 tablespoons honey
40g self-raising flour
40g plain flour
Pinch of bicarbonate of soda
Pinch of salt
25g cocoa
50g ground almonds
250g raw finely grated beetroot
100ml beetroot juice reduction (reduced from 200ml)
30ml sunflower oil

BEETROOT HONEYCOMB:

75g honey
140g glucose
400g caster sugar
5 tablespoons beetroot juice reduction (reduced from 10 tablespoons)
20g bicarbonate of soda
Melted chocolate to coat

Method

For the cake:

Whisk the sugar, salt, honey, treacle and egg in an electric mixer until the ingredients double in size.

Fold in the flour, cocoa, almonds and bicarbonate.

Fold in the beetroot, chocolate, beetroot juice and oil.

Bake for 1 hour at 140°c in a large cake ring.

For the cinder toffee:

Boil the honey, glucose, sugar and beetroot juice in a heavy-based saucepan till it reaches 150°c on a sugar thermometer.

Sieve the bicarbonate twice and add to mix.

Stir through quickly then pour onto baking tray lined with a Silpat (a non-stick baking mat).

Once cooled, break into small pieces and dip into the chocolate.

Chef's Secret

This recipe may sound unusual but it really works as the sweetness of the beetroot balances the bitterness of the chocolate.

Chocolate and frangipane cake with figs, red wine ripple ice cream, red wine syrup and crushed hazelnuts

Serves 6

Ingredients

FOR THE CAKE:

250g ground almonds
150g hazelnuts, crushed
250g butter
250g icing sugar
3 eggs
2 egg yolks
50g plain flour
50g cocoa powder

For the ice cream see our basic recipe on page 160

FOR A RED WINE SYRUP:

500ml red wine
200g caster sugar

TO GARNISH:

12 figs cut in half
Handfull of hazelnuts, crushed

Method

To make the cake:
Cream the butter and sugar with an electric whisk until light and fluffy. Add the almonds, flour and cocoa and whisk in, followed by the eggs (one at a time) and whisk in. Add the crushed hazelnuts. Place in a baking tray lined with baking parchment and bake at 150ºc for 45 minutes-1 hour.

First make a red wine syrup:
Place the wine and sugar in a saucepan and reduce by two thirds until a thick syrup, save a little back for decorating the dish.

To assemble:
Place fig halves on the top of each cake portion, drizzle the red wine syrup on the plate, sprinkle crushed hazelnuts around then add a scoop of the red wine ripple ice cream.

Poached pears with mulled wine, lemon balm ice cream and mulled wine shot

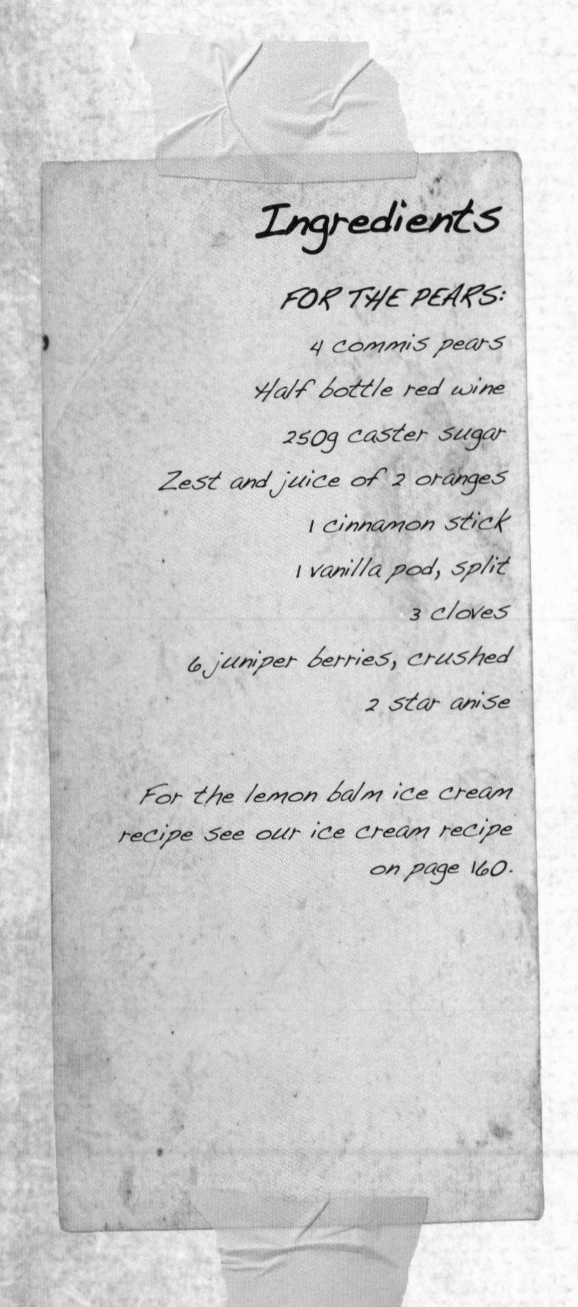

Ingredients

FOR THE PEARS:

4 commis pears

Half bottle red wine

250g caster sugar

Zest and juice of 2 oranges

1 cinnamon stick

1 vanilla pod, split

3 cloves

6 juniper berries, crushed

2 star anise

For the lemon balm ice cream recipe see our ice cream recipe on page 160.

Method

For the pears:

Peel and core the pears. Place all the remaining ingredients in a saucepan and bring to the boil. Turn down to a simmer and allow to infuse for 30 minutes.

Add the pears and cover with a sheet of baking parchment. Simmer the pears for 20 minutes. Take off the heat and allow the pears to cool in the liquid.

Place the pears in the fridge with the cooking liquid and allow to infuse for 24 hours.

Rhubarb Trio

Rhubarb crumble, ginger cake milk shake with rhubarb crisps served with rhubarb and orange ice cream.

Ingredients

FOR THE CRUMBLE TOPPING:
50g butter, cubed
100g flour
75g caster sugar
Half a vanilla pod

FOR THE RHUBARB CRUMBLE FILLING:
200g rhubarb
150g caster sugar
1 tablespoon water
Juice of half a lemon

FOR THE GINGER CAKE MILK SHAKE:
150ml semi-skimmed milk
50g double cream
1 tablespoon liquid glucose
50g Jamaican ginger cake
1 teaspoon lecithin
30g caster sugar

FOR THE RHUBARB CRISPS:
2 sticks rhubarb
40g sugar
40ml water
Juice of half a lemon

See our ice cream recipe on page 160 for the rhubarb and orange ice cream

Method

For the crumble topping:

Remove the seeds from the vanilla pod and place in a bowl with the butter and flour. Rub together until the mixture resembles fine breadcrumbs. Add the sugar and mix in well.

For the rhubarb crumble filling:

Chop the rhubarb into 2cm cubes and place in a saucepan with the remaining ingredients. Cook over a medium heat until the rhubarb is cooked. Taste for sweetness – if the rhubarb is especially sour, add extra sugar.

Place the rhubarb in the bottom of an ovenproof ramekin and top with the crumble mix. Place in a pre-heated oven at 170oc for 15-20 minutes until the crumble is golden and piping hot.

For the ginger cake milk shake:

Place all the ingredients in a saucepan and crumble in the ginger cake. Bring to the boil then turn down the heat and allow to simmer for 20 minutes.

Remove from the heat and allow all the ingredients to infuse for 1 hour. Transfer to a bar blender and blend until smooth. Pass through a fine sieve and then chill.

For the rhubarb crisps:

Place the sugar, water and lemon juice in a saucepan and bring to the boil. Turn down the heat and simmer until thickened slightly. Using a speed peeler or mandolin, peel off long thin strips of the rhubarb.

Dip the strips in the sugar syrup and place on a baking tray lined with baking parchment. Bake in the oven at 70°c. If your oven will not operate so low, switch it on pilot and allow to dry until crisp. This should take about 2 hours.

Trio of strawberry

Strawberry and cream terrine, strawberry shortbread, and a strawberry fab.

Ingredients

FOR THE TERRINE:

FOR THE STRAWBERRY PURÉE:

500g strawberries, quartered
100ml water
150g caster sugar
2 and a half gelatine leaves

FOR THE CREAM LAYER:

Half pint double cream
Handful of mint leaves
2 and a half gelatine leaves

FOR THE STRAWBERRY SHORTBREAD:

60g caster sugar
2 large egg yolks
60g butter
85g strong bread flour
1 level teaspoon baking powder
Seeds from half a vanilla pod
Strawberries for topping

BALSAMIC REDUCTION:

100ml balsamic vinegar
50ml caster sugar

STRAWBERRY FAB:

300g Strawberry purée (made in the same way as the purée for the terrine)
300g double cream
70g egg yolks
50g caster sugar
50g hundreds and thousands

Method

To make the strawberry and cream terrine:
For the strawberry layer:
Cook the strawberries to a pulp with the sugar and water. Blend in a blender then pass through a sieve to make a fine purée. The purée should be the consistency of double cream.
Soak two and a half gelatine leaves in cold water for 10 minutes to allow to soften. Take the gelatine out of the water and squeeze out any excess water.
Gently bring the purée to the boil in a saucepan and then add the soaked gelatine.
Whisk and allow the gelatine to dissolve, then pass the mix through a fine strainer.

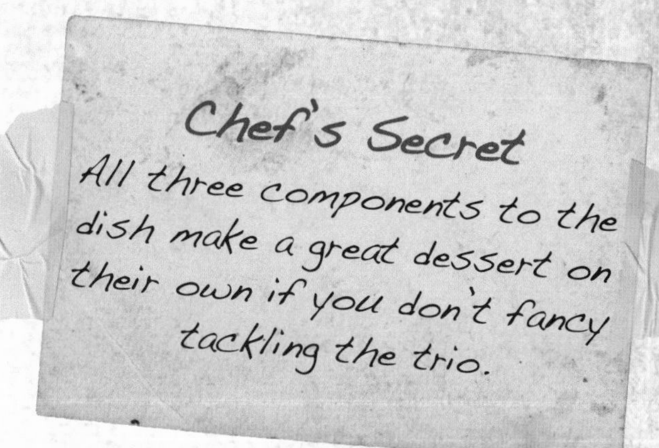

For the cream:
Soak two and a half gelatine leaves in cold water for 10 minutes to allow to soften. Take the gelatine out of the water and squeeze out and excess water. Meanwhile place the cream and mint in a saucepan and bring to the boil. Once boiled, take off the heat and allow to infuse for one hour. Pass the mixture through a strainer to remove the mint leaves and then bring 100ml of the liquid to the boil. Add the soaked gelatine leaves, whisk to dissolve and then place the mix thorough a strainer.
To assemble the terrine:
Line a terrine mould with a layer of cling film ensuring no air bubbles remain and that the cling film is perfectly smooth in the mould as any creases will show when the terrine is sliced.
Pour a layer of the strawberry purée 1cm deep into the terrine mould. Place in the fridge and allow to set fully.
Once the strawberry layer is set, pour on a 1cm layer of the cream mixture and allow to set in the fridge for an hour. When set, repeat with the strawberry and then cream until you have all 4 layers. Keep the terrine in the fridge until ready to serve and then slice with a hot knife at 1cm intervals.
For the strawberry shortbread:
In a food processor, blend the sugar and butter until light and creamy. Add the eggs and vanilla and whisk in. Sift the flour and baking powder and add to the mix. Beat to combine into a dough. Place the dough in cling film and roll up into a sausage shape.
Place the dough in the freezer for 3 hours (It's easier to slice neat circles from frozen).
Slice the shortbreads into half centimetre thick rounds and then place on a baking tray lined with baking parchment. Bake in a pre-heated oven at 150°c for 10-15 minutes. Place carefully on a cooling rack and allow to cool.
To make the balsamic reduction:
Place the ingredients in a pan and then bring to the boil, reduce by about half until you have a thick glossy syrup.
For the strawberry fab:
Place the cream and strawberry in a saucepan and bring to the boil, then immediately remove from the heat.
Whisk the yolks and sugar together until light and pale. Add a small amount of the cream and strawberry mixture to the sugar and egg yolks and whisk together. Repeat with the remaining mixture a little at a time. Place in a clean pan.
On a medium heat, simmer the mixture stirring constantly. Being careful to ensure none sticks to the bottom of the pan, cook until it thickens (the mixture is ready when it coats the back of a wooden spoon). Do not allow the mix to come to the boil otherwise the eggs will scramble and the texture will be unpalatable.
Once cooled, divide the mixture between small dariole moulds or shot glasses and transfer to the freezer until frozen.
To unmould, dip the frozen mould or shot glasses in warm water to loosen. Coat in the hundreds and thousands.
To assemble:
Place a slice of the terrine on a chilled plate. Put a fresh strawberry on the shortbread and then drizzle with the balsamic syrup before adding the strawberry fab.

White chocolate pavé and cherries, sherry and maple syrup reduction

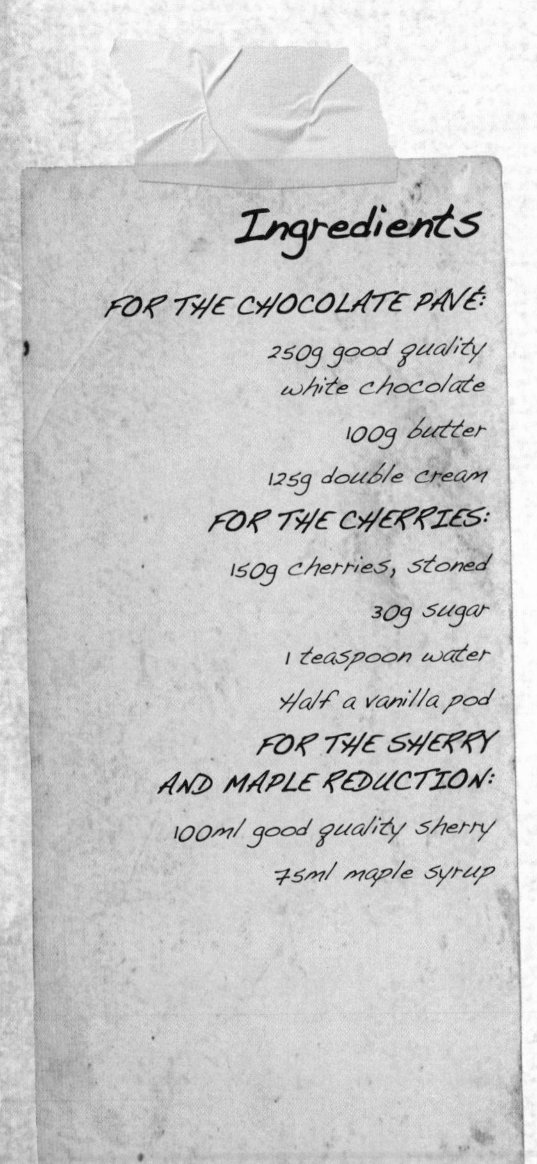

Ingredients

FOR THE CHOCOLATE PAVÉ:

250g good quality white chocolate

100g butter

125g double cream

FOR THE CHERRIES:

150g cherries, stoned

30g sugar

1 teaspoon water

Half a vanilla pod

FOR THE SHERRY AND MAPLE REDUCTION:

100ml good quality sherry

75ml maple syrup

Method

For the chocolate pavé:

Place a metal bowl over a pan of simmering water and slowly melt the chocolate and cream together, ensuring they are fully combined.

Cut the butter into small cubes. Take the cream and chocolate mixture off the heat and whisk in the butter until fully incorporated.

Pour into a shallow container lined with clingfilm and allow to fully set in the fridge. With a hot knife, cut into large slabs.

For the cherries:

Place all the ingredients in a saucepan and then cook over a moderate heat until the liquid is dissolved. The cherries should still be whole but soft.

For the sherry and maple reduction:

Place the maple syrup and sherry in a saucepan and reduce down by half until a thick syrup.

To assemble:

Spoon some of the maple and sherry syrup onto a plate. Place the pavé on the plate and arrange the cherries. Garnish with a few sprigs of lemon balm or mint.

The Milestone Basic Recipes

Beef stock

1kg beef bones
2 carrots, roughly chopped
2 onions, quartered
2 sticks celery, roughly chopped
1 tablespoon vegetable oil
8 peppercorns
2 dried bay leaves
3-4 fresh parsley stalks
1 sprig fresh thyme

Heat the oven to 200oc.

Put the bones in a roasting tin and bake until well browned.

Put the carrot, onion and celery in another roasting tin and toss in the oil. Bake until well browned.

Put the vegetables and the bones in a large pan and add the peppercorns, bay leaves, parsley and thyme. Cover with water.

Bring to the boil and skim off any scum that has formed. Cover and simmer very gently for 3-4 hours. From time to time, skim off any scum that forms. Strain into a large bowl and allow to cool. Chill overnight. Skim off any fat that has formed on the surface.

Piccalilli

This is about as far away from the stuff you buy in a jar as Sheffield is from John O'Groats.

Next time you're up in Scotland, take some to have with your oatcakes and cheese

400g pearl onions
250g carrots
500g cauliflower
250g diced apple
150g sweetcorn
250g cucumber
650ml vinegar
Half tablespoon turmeric
Half tablespoon coriander seeds
15g crushed garlic
125g sugar
3 cardamom pods
2.5 tablespoon cornflour
1 teaspoon salt
150g wholegrain mustard
150g olive oil

Boil the olive oil, mustard, salt, cardamom, sugar, garlic, coriander, turmeric and vinegar in a saucepan.

Chop the vegetables into 1cm dice and break the cauliflowers into small florets of similar size.

Take 2 tablespoons of the liquid and mix with the cornflour into a smooth paste.

Add a small amount of the hot liquid to the cornflour mixture and whisk until combined.

Return to the heat and allow to thicken.

Add the remaining ingredients and bring to the boil.

Once boiled, take off the heat and allow to cool.

This will keep for 3 months if correctly stored in a sterilised Kilner or jam jar.

New Vanguard • 99

Space Shuttle L[illegible] System 1972–2004

Mark Lardas • Illustrated by Ian Palmer

First published in Great Britain in 2004 by Osprey Publishing, Elms Court,
Chapel Way, Botley, Oxford OX2 9LP, United Kingdom.
Email: info@ospreypublishing.com

A CIP catalogue record for this book is available from the British Library.

ISBN 1 84176 691 7

Editor: Simone Drinkwater
Design: Ken Vail Graphic Design, Cambridge, UK
Index by Alison Worthington
Originated by The Electronic Page Company, Cwmbran, UK
Printed in China through World Print Ltd.

04 05 06 07 08 10 9 8 7 6 5 4 3 2 1

For a catalog of all books published by Osprey Military
and Aviation please contact:

Osprey Direct USA, c/o MBI Publishing, P.O. Box 1,
729 Prospect Ave, Osceola, WI 54020, USA
E-mail: info@ospreydirectusa.com

Osprey Direct UK, P.O. Box 140, Wellingborough,
Northants, NN8 2FA, UK
E-mail: info@ospreydirect.co.uk

www.ospreypublishing.com

Author's dedication

This book is dedicated to Robert Howarton – model-maker extraordinaire and Shuttle fan.

Author's note

All illustrations in this book, unless otherwise credited, were provided by the National Astronautics and Space Administration (NASA).

Artist's note

Readers may care to note that prints of the original paintings from which the color plates in this book were prepared are available for private sale. All reproduction copyright whatsoever is retained by the Publishers. All enquiries should be addressed to:

Ian Palmer, 15 Floriston Avenue, Hillingdon, Middlesex, UB10 9DZ, UK

The Publishers regret that they can enter into no correspondence upon this matter.

SPACE SHUTTLE LAUNCH SYSTEM 1972–2004

INTRODUCTION

It was a stock techno-thriller subplot in the 1970s and 1980s: a Space Shuttle launch during a fictional Third World War – an Air Force Shuttle, launched on a military mission to help the United States win the war. Frequently, these stories involved the Shuttle in combat – the first-ever space combat. Sometimes the Orbiter won its fictional encounter. More often, it was destroyed.

Reality followed a different course. Military use of the Shuttle has been tentative, reluctant, and fleeting. Operational shortcomings, rather than military action, have caused Shuttle losses. Rather than being an orbital bomber or daring spy plane, the Shuttle has been a space-age dump truck, a high-tech 18-wheeler.

The Shuttle was conceived when space was seen as the new high ground. It was thought that those who commanded space could keep the rest of the world's nations penned on Earth, much as Nelson's navy kept Revolutionary France trapped on the European continent. Its design shows the influence of a perceived military role: the size of the payload bay, the maximum weight of any payload delivered to orbit it was designed to carry, even its double-delta wing sprang from the military missions it was intended to support.

When the Shuttle finally flew, new realities emerged. The new high ground proved a vulnerable ridgeline, where you could be picked off by invisible enemies hidden in undergrowth. Manned space flight was as public as Times Square on New Year's Day, complicating clandestine operations. Space is an incredibly hostile environment, better fit for electronic robots than human beings, and many uses of space – such as the Global Positioning System – had not been conceived in the late 1960s when the Shuttle design began.

The Space Transportation System – consisting of an orbital space plane, solid booster rockets, and an external fuel tank – was a compromise, with all the limitations that compromises often entail. It has proved less satisfactory than its champions promised. It never delivered a once-a-week launch rate, polar launch capabilities, or even a payload of 65,000lb into low-Earth orbit. It is more expensive than expendable launch vehicles.

Replicas of Christopher Columbus' ships sail past the Orbiter *Endeavour* at Launch Pad 39B as *Endeavour* awaits liftoff on its maiden voyage, STS-49. Photographed during the Columbus quincentennial in June 1992, it illustrates the link between explorers throughout time.

Despite its limitations the Shuttle remains revolutionary. Both it and the spacecraft deployed from it are still the only successful reusable spacecraft. The Shuttle gives humans unprecedented access to low-Earth orbit, allowing ordinary individuals to travel in space. Remarkably flexible, it has made projects like the International Space Station (ISS), the Hubble Space Telescope (HST), and Long Duration Experiment Facility (LDEF) possible.

DESIGN AND DEVELOPMENT

Genesis

In 1969 man reached the Moon and the National Aeronautics and Space Administration (NASA), began to consider its next major endeavor. A manned space station seemed achievable, if transportation costs to low-Earth orbit could be reduced. A reusable launching system – a space shuttle – promised the requisite savings, so NASA proposed a combined station/shuttle initiative.

The initial shuttle design proposed by Maxime Faget, NASA's chief designer, was completely reusable. A manned, fly-back first stage that was the size of a Boeing 747 airliner, but could out-perform an X-15, would launch, carrying an Orbiter. At staging, the Orbiter, which would be larger than a 707 airliner, would launch from the first stage. The first stage would turn around, and fly back to the launch pad. Both first stage and Orbiter had straight wings allowing them to glide to a landing on a conventional runway at airline speeds. Liquid-fueled rockets would power both, and the system could carry a small (20,000–30,000lb) payload.

It was too expensive. NASA could get funding for one of the two projects and about half of the other. Neither project could be justified in isolation: without a space shuttle, a space station could not be maintained. Without a space station, there was insufficient justification for a space shuttle. Seeking extra funds, NASA approached the Air Force.

By 1970 the United States Air Force (USAF) had been striving for a manned military presence for nearly a decade. Two manned programs – Dyna-Soar and the Manned Orbiting Laboratory (MOL) – had been started and then abandoned. Dyna-Soar, a manned orbital spaceplane

This model – currently on display at Johnson Space Center – shows the original Shuttle concept: a manned fly-back first stage, and a straight-winged Orbiter, capable of landing at airliner speeds. (Author's collection)

The Manned Orbital Laboratory (MOL) was the military's second effort to create a manned military presence in space. The program was canceled in 1969, and the seven astronauts assigned to it were transferred to NASA. Ironically, they provided commanders for most of the first Shuttle missions – another program that started as a military effort, but ended being transferred to civilian use.

initially intended as an orbital bomber, evolved into a payload delivery system before cancellation in 1964. MOL, a manned reconnaissance platform, had been abandoned the previous year, in 1969. The seven astronauts were reassigned to NASA. When NASA offered the Air Force a chance to get back into manned space flight, the Air Force was interested.

Air Force–NASA partnerships were common. The X-15 and XB-70 mach-3 bomber were joint Air Force–NASA projects. NASA's launch facilities at Cape Canaveral, Florida, as well as facilities at White Sands (New Mexico) and Edwards Air Force Base (California), were shared with the Air Force, as was the joint research on lifting bodies and hypersonic aircraft performance; the Air Force sometimes provided the funding for these projects. NASA obtained aircraft used to support this research from the Air Force. The Air Force MOL used a militarized version of the NASA's Gemini manned space capsule. A jointly developed shuttle seemed natural.

The Air Force knew that without its support NASA would not get a space shuttle. Reconnaissance was a major space military mission and the United States' principal foe, the Soviet Union, had significant bases in the Arctic. To fly over all of the Soviet Union American military reconnaissance satellites needed high-inclination orbits.

The Earth's rotation assists spacecraft launching due east. Increasing an orbit's inclination reduces this assistance. Launches due north (or south) get no rotational assistance. With launch inclinations in excess of 90° the Earth's rotation reduces the speed of the vehicle. A launch system that puts 30,000lb into orbit launched due east may only carry a 5,000lb payload into the 97° inclination orbit required for observation. The Air Force already planned optical reconnaissance satellites – the Keyhole series – that weighed up to 40,000lb. These required a payload bay that was 15ft across and 60ft in length. Upgraded (by means of adding larger solid rocket boosters) Titan III boosters could place these into a 97° inclination orbit. Faget's design could not.

The Earth's rotation moves the launch site after launch. A rocket launched from the United States crosses roughly 1,100 nautical miles west of its launch site when it has completed one orbit. Due to range safety, satellites requiring inclinations greater than 65° were launched on the Pacific coast, from Vandenberg Air Force Base. This put a spacecraft over the Pacific Ocean after completing one orbit.

To land on American soil – critical for classified military payloads – the Air Force required the ability to fly crossrange (perpendicular to the direction of the orbit) 1,100 nautical miles. The Air Force also planned missions that were to be completed in one orbit. The vehicle would go

By Authority to Proceed, the Orbiter design had evolved to a double-delta wing, but one with twin rudders, raised wing tips, and jet engines for landing. This was a heat transfer model of the design used by Rockwell to refine the craft. (Author's collection)

up, launch or retrieve a payload, then return to Earth at an American military facility. Faget's design had less than 200 miles of crossrange capability, and was thus impractical for the military.

The Shuttle design was altered to accommodate Air Force requirements. The larger payload bay and the increased payload – 65,000lb when launched due east – increased the size of the entire system. A double-delta design was adapted – with a broad triangle forming the wings and a narrow triangle merging the wing to the fuselage. The double delta improved performance at hypersonic speeds – this increased both crossrange capability and vehicle heating during reentry. Additionally, a delta wing has a higher sink rate and stall speed. Faget's straight-winged craft landed at a stately 130 knots. A delta design sizzled down the runway at 190 knots.

Budgetary pressures further complicated these requirements. Previous aerospace craft operating in hypersonic environments, such as the X-15, were made from titanium, using the titanium structure as a heat sink. A "hot-structure" Orbiter would have been the largest titanium airframe ever constructed, and consequently, fantastically expensive.

However, a new insulator was being developed – silica tiles. The insulating silica was light, would not oxidize, and could withstand temperatures up to 2,500°F. This promised a reusable insulation that permitted an aluminum-frame vehicle. It was much less expensive than titanium. Not surprisingly, NASA opted for this thermal tile system.

NASA also reduced costs by substituting strap-on boosters for the fly-back first stage. Initially these were liquid-fueled, but the costs and complexity of liquid-fueled boosters prompted NASA to investigate the use of solid rockets.

Solids were cheap and reliable, burning a mixture of powdered aluminum and ammonium perchloride oxidizer. Their thrust was comparable to that obtainable with liquid oxygen and kerosene, a common rocket fuel. Although the proposed Shuttle would require solids larger than those used before, a solid rocket booster would cost much less than a liquid booster. The solid rocket casings would also be sturdy enough to be retrieved and reused.

Once lit, however, solid rocket boosters (SRBs) burned until they were exhausted. Aborting a launch while they were burning was impossible. All previous manned spacecraft used liquid-fueled engines that could be throttled. NASA chose to accept the risk inherent with SRBs.

NASA contracted for a new motor for the planned Shuttle fueled with liquid oxygen-liquid hydrogen (LO_2-LH_2). Initially they demanded an engine that could generate 415,000lb of thrust, with a motor that was to be reusable and throttleable. After Air Force requirements increased the payload to 65,000lb, NASA changed the engine requirements to 550,000lb of thrust.

The liquid hydrogen and oxygen fuel affected the vehicle design. Liquid hydrogen is bulky and makes up one-seventh of the total fuel weight in a LO_2-LH_2 system, while accounting for three-fourths of the volume. It is light, however, and can be stored in lightweight tanks. Proposals were drafted for storing liquid hydrogen in disposable, external tanks. The proposed Orbiter shrank.

NASA finally put all of the liquid fuel in an external tank, producing the configuration used today. The orbiting spacecraft would be built from aluminum with a silica-tile thermal protection system. Launched with LO_2-LH_2 engines, it would use double-delta wings for reentry and draw fuel from a large external tank. Attached to the external tank, two solid rocket boosters provided the first stage impetus.

A painful birth

NASA had its design. Success depended upon coordinated completion of several disparate technologies. Both propulsion systems were unprecedented. The Space Shuttle Main Engine (SSME) was larger than any comparable LO_2-LH_2 engine, throttleable and reuseable. The SRBs were so big that, unlike any of their predecessors, they had to be built in sections. While the aluminum structure simplified construction, that gamble was predicated on an untested thermal tile.

NASA's proposal arrived as the United States' economy experienced "stagflation" – economic stagnation combined with inflation. NASA funding came from the discretionary budget – the small fraction of the Congressional spending that could be cut. Always on the budget chopping block, NASA starved its other programs to fund the Shuttle – abandoning the space station, and canceling three Apollo Moon missions.

NASA used extravagant claims to sell the Shuttle: they declared that the Shuttle would make space flight as routine as a bus ride; it could launch once a week; a fleet of four Orbiters would complete 400 missions in ten years; every object placed in orbit would start into space aboard the Shuttle. Based on an economic analysis conducted in 1970, the Shuttle would recoup development costs after 506 launches, and on its next 400 missions NASA would clear a profit.

The numbers were based on optimistic assumptions – that the Shuttle would increase demand for space by cutting costs of access, that enough payloads would exist to ensure each Shuttle launch was full, that inflation remained under control. Most importantly, it assumed development would

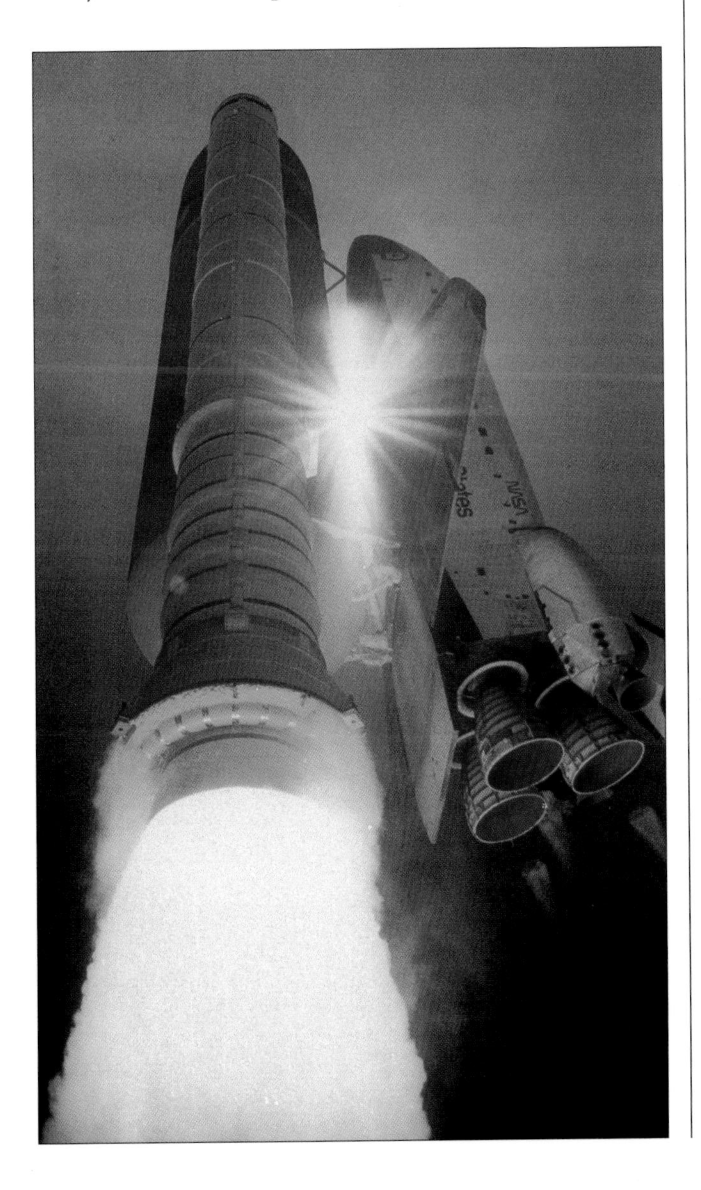

The difference between the SRBs and SSMEs can be clearly seen in this view of a Shuttle launch. The solid fuel – a mixture of powdered aluminum and ammonium perchloride – burns with a bright white flame. The liquid-hydrogen and liquid-oxygen of the SSMEs yields an almost-invisible blue flame.

follow schedules. Any slip – whether due to development difficulties or budget cuts – upset the coordination of several mutually dependent and technically challenging development programs. The Shuttle experienced both budget and developmental problems.

The Space Shuttle Main Engine (SSME) proved the first hurdle. Pratt and Whitney, the losing bidder, challenged the contract awarded to Rocketdyne in 1971. Engine development stopped until the challenge was settled, in 1972. The Main Propulsion Test Article (MPTA-098) – used to test the Space Shuttle Main Engines – only began construction in 1974. The SSMEs proved to be the program's laggard child, delaying the first launch by at least six months.

NASA awarded the Orbiter contract to Rockwell International (formerly North American Aviation) in August 1972. Rockwell was also named the system integrator. Martin (later Martin-Marietta) won the External Tank contract, and built it at their New Orleans, LA factory. Marshall Space Flight Center (MSFC), a NASA center, retained responsibility for integration and final assembly of the Solid Rocket Booster, parceling the contracts for the structure to McDonnell Douglas Astronautics in Huntington Beach, CA, and the rocket motors to Thiokol (later Morton-Thiokol) in Wasach, UT.

Rockwell divided the Orbiter contract among major aerospace manufacturers in the United States. Rockwell used Orbiter structural groups – major subassemblies – as the partitions. Grumman (now Northrup-Grumman) in Beth Page, NY, received the subcontract for the wings, General Dynamics in San Diego, CA, built the mid-body, and McDonnell Douglas, in St. Louis, MO, developed the Orbital Maneuvering System and the aft Reaction Control System. The Shuttle was now dispersed throughout the country. If Congress canceled the program the effects would be felt in many Congressional Districts.

The Shuttle required new launch and processing facilities. NASA began converting the two Saturn launch pads and Saturn support buildings, such as the Vehicle Assembly Building (VAB) at the Kennedy

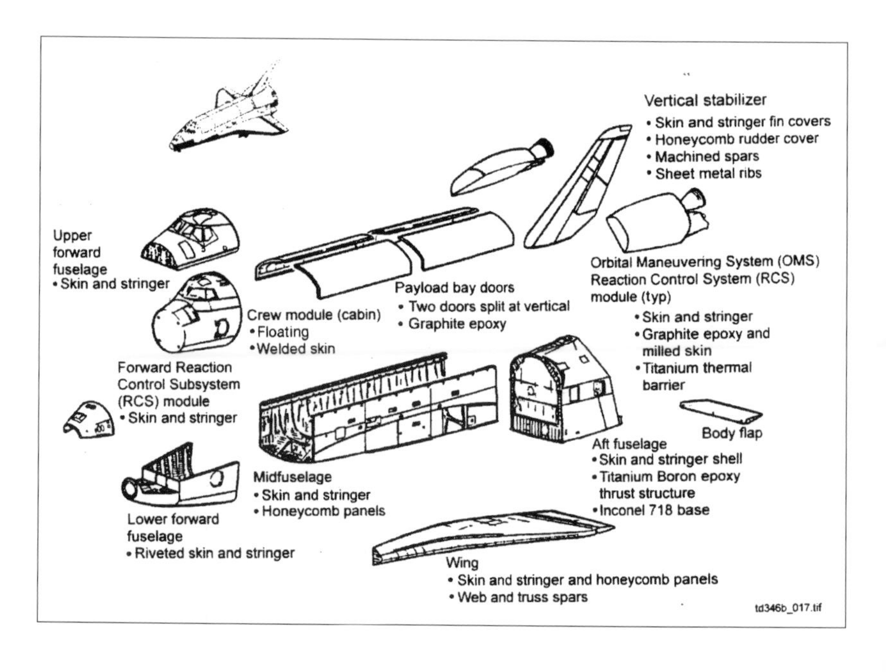

The Orbiter consists of 16 major structural groups. This modular approach allowed NASA to convert a high-fidelity structural test assembly and a collection of operational spares into the Orbiters *Challenger* and *Endeavour*.

Space Center (KSC) for Shuttle use. The Air Force agreed to convert their never-completed MOL launch pad at Vandenberg AFB – Space Launch Complex 6 (SLC-6) – for polar Shuttle launches.

Other facilities were needed. To reduce costs, the SRBs would parachute to a soft landing, then be recovered and refurbished. NASA let contracts for two recovery ships – *Liberty* and *Freedom* – as well as SRB refurbishment facilities.

Transporting the Orbiter was a problem. Unless it always landed at KSC or Vandenberg – which was unlikely given uncooperative weather or an emergency landing situation – a means of transporting the Orbiter was required. It was too large to travel by road, and moving it by water was too slow – and you could not guarantee all contingency landings would be made close to waterways.

The solution came from the test program. Drop tests, simulating an entry were necessary, and it became clear that the Orbiter could be carried atop a 747 aircraft. A 747 was leased and modified for the drop tests. NASA realized they had their transporter. The 747 was retained, and a second was purchased in the 1980s.

NASA contracted for permanent mate-demate facilities (to separate or join the Orbiter to the 747 transporter) at KSC, Vandenberg, and Dryden-Edwards, as well as an air-portable mate-demate mechanism for contingencies.

From prototype to flight

In 1972 Rockwell had contractual authority to produce two Shuttle Orbiter Vehicles, a Main Propulsion Test Article (MPTA-098), and a Structural Test Article (STA-099). The Orbiter Vehicles, then unnamed, were OV-101 (*Enterprise*) and OV-102 (*Columbia*). Both were intended as operational Orbiters.

MPTA-098 replicated the structure of the main propulsion system and was to be used to prove the Space Shuttle Main Engine (SSME).

STA-099 was a high-fidelity structural replica of the Orbiter vehicle. It contained a boilerplate crew compartment, but would be otherwise identical to the flying vehicles. It would be used for structural, vibration, and pressure testing.

The conventional aluminum structure allowed construction of the first Orbiters to progress rapidly. The airframe of OV-101, started in June 1974, was essentially completed by September 1976 – well before the rest of the system required for flight, and before the infrastructure needed for basic operations was ready. Systems required for space flight, such as the SSMEs and OMS/RCS pods, were incomplete at *Enterprise*'s rollout to Dryden. Aerodynamic dummies were installed to make *Enterprise* available for necessary pre-launch testing in advance of space flight.

Development of the SRBs – despite their unprecedented size – also came together swiftly. Thiokol, the motor developer, had beaten Aerojet, a Florida-based company, to win the competition for the SRBs. Aerojet lost despite proposing a monolithic motor – one solid piece of fuel. Thiokol's design used a segmented SRB. Three sections of propellant would be stacked, then mated together at a launch site processing building.

Building the engines in segments simplified transportation – which was significant when SRBs had to be shipped to two launch sites separated by a continent. Aerojet's monolithic motor would have to be barged, simple

enough when shipping to KSC at Cape Canaveral, but more problematic when sending motors to Vandenberg, California. Thiokol held the first test firing of an SRB on July 18, 1977 followed by two more the next year.

The conversion of KSC facilities progressed satisfactorily. While still supporting Saturn launches in 1975, new construction and facility conversion proceeded swiftly enough to support Shuttle activities at the end of 1978. The Vehicle Assembly Building was ready by the summer of 1978, launch pad 39-A had been converted by December 1978, and Mission Control in January 1979. Pad 39-B would not be finished until late 1985. NASA was ready for launch operations on schedule.

ABOVE **One of the few times that two Orbiters were on launch pads simultaneously awaiting launch occurred in July 2001.**

Other parts faired more poorly. The Air Force began converting SLC-6 (or "Slick Six") in 1979, late for launches planned in the early 1980s. At Kennedy NASA converted facilities built for the Saturn, a rocket larger than the Shuttle. SLC-6 was originally intended as a launch site for a smaller vehicle, the Titan III, and the conversion spiraled into a succession of modifications and alterations in an ultimately unsuccessful attempt to match SLC-6 to the Shuttle. The facility was unfinished in 1986, when the *Challenger* accident halted Shuttle launches.

SSME development, which started late, continued to run late. The first test firing of an SSME occurred in December 1976. MPTA-098 was installed at the National Space Technology Laboratory, in Bay St. Louis, Mississippi, by autumn 1977, with a first test firing in April 1978. Frustrating test failures followed – shutdowns, turbopump failures, a fractured valve that caused structural damage. It was not until January 1981 – two years after the planned 1979 first lift-off date – that the SSMEs successfully completed a full flight demonstration.

BELOW **A test firing of the SSME in May 1981 at the National Space Technology Laboratories in Mississippi. Developing reliable SSMEs delayed the Shuttle program more than any other single factor.**

Thermal tile system production also lagged. The tiles used for *Columbia*'s first flight were not completely delivered and installed until a few weeks before the first launch.

Originally *Enterprise* was to be returned to Downey for conversion to flight status, after integrated ground vibration tests held at MSFC in 1978. However, after design evolution while *Enterprise* was undergoing testing, the flight vehicle was considerably different to the Orbiter that had emerged from Downey in 1975. *Enterprise*'s conversion was deemed uneconomical, and canceled, which would have left NASA without a second Orbiter until 1984, when follow-on Orbiters were planned. NASA instead converted STA-099 to flight status, replacing the boilerplate crew compartment with a flight article. Conversion began in 1979. STA-099 became OV-099, *Challenger*.

Evolution in the flight era

Even after the Shuttle's first flight in April 1981, it remained an experimental vehicle, under development. NASA awarded Rockwell a contract for two additional vehicles, OV-102 (*Discovery*) and OV-103 (*Atlantis*) in 1979, along with *Challenger.* The two new vehicles saw significant improvements over the first Orbiters. They were structurally lighter, and substituted thermal blankets for tiles over the low heat areas. *Discovery* and *Atlantis* were nearly 8,000lb lighter than *Columbia,* the equivalent of a standard commercial satellite.

NASA also continued development of the External Tanks. Initially, the ETs weighed 77,000lb. A new lightweight ET was introduced in 1983, which weighed 66,000lb, increasing available payload by 10,000lb. In 1998, a super-lightweight tank was introduced. Made from aluminum-lithium alloy, it reduced tank weight, increased cargo weight by an additional 7,500lb, and is 30% stronger than the lightweight tanks.

NASA developed three new upper stages for use with the Orbiter. The Payload Assist Module (PAM) and Inertial Upper Stage (IUS) were solid-fueled transfer stages intended to put payloads into higher orbit. A PAM could hoist a 500–1,400lb payload into geostationary orbit (an orbit with a 24-hr period, that remained in the same spot over the Earth as the earth rotates). The IUS could place a 5,000lb satellite into geostationary orbit. Both were used successfully after initially experiencing embarrassing failures.

The Centaur upper stage was a high-energy, liquid-fueled (LO_2-LH_2) booster developed to allow the Orbiter to launch interplanetary probes, but it was never used aboard the Orbiter. Development fell behind. Its first operational use was scheduled for spring 1986, when launch windows opened for a Jupiter and Saturn mission. The Centaur was already controversial because its cryogenic fuel had to be dumped prior to landing in a launch abort. Engineers were uneasy as to the effect of venting flammable fuel while the engines were thrusting the Shuttle to a landing site. Additionally, the Orbiter lacked the plumbing to dump all of the Centaur's fuel by the time the Orbiter landed when performing the shortest aborts. After the 1986 *Challenger* accident, the Shuttle-Centaur was canceled.

Following *Challenger,* NASA made a number of changes to the Shuttle. The most significant was the redesign of the SRB field joints, where the SRB segments mated together. Hot gasses escaping from a joint destroyed the Shuttle, so a more robust joint was added, with a stronger tang and clevis structure, and longer pins to preclude gas leakage.

Other nagging problems were also resolved. Improved Auxiliary Power Units (APUs) were developed. These lasted three times longer than the old units. Improved disconnects

Three completed lightweight ETs at the Michoud assembly plant awaiting delivery to KSC in 1981.

Deployment of a TDRSS satellite from the Orbiter. A spring-loaded platform in the harness holding the satellite in the cargo bay pushes the satellite out of the Orbiter. An IUS upper stage (white portion on bottom) then boosts the satellite (gold and black upper portion) to a geostationary orbit.

for the Space Shuttle Main Engine (SSME) fuel lines were added. With the previous disconnects, inadvertent closure of the valve connecting the Orbiter to the ET (external tank) could have caused a catastrophic failure.

Other changes included the addition of a drag parachute, to shorten the Oribiter's roll-out following landing, a steerable nose wheel, to increase control on landing, upgraded brakes, and a crew escape system. The crew escape system allows the crew hatch to be opened in flight, and the crew to bail out once the Orbiter vehicle is in subsonic flight. It is useful only when a problem precludes an intact Orbiter landing, but allows the Orbiter to survive through most of reentry.

After the *Challenger* accident, NASA ordered a replacement Orbiter. Built from structural spares ordered in 1983, it became the Orbiter *Endeavour*, and incorporated the post-*Challenger* changes.

Alterations in the 1990s included an Extended Duration package that allowed 30-day missions, a "glass cockpit" that upgrades the flight avionics from a 1970s standard to current state-of-the-art, and a relocated airlock, allowing the Orbiters to dock with the International Space Station.

Rivals and replacements

The Shuttle remains the world's only reusable launch system, although the Soviet Union came closest to duplicating it. They did not believe a rival would spend billions developing the Shuttle unless national security was involved and thought that the economic analysis used to justify the Shuttle was completely phony. They regarded the involvement of the United States Air Force with suspicion, and believed that NASA provided cover stories for previous Air Force military activities: the U-2 spy plane, for example, was once passed off as a NASA research aircraft.

The Soviets knew the Shuttle must have a military purpose beyond satellite delivery – they just could not determine what it was. Their best guess was that it was a hypersonic bomber, intended to strike high value targets in the Soviet Union. To learn what the Shuttle was for, they felt they had to build one.

In 1976 Brezhnev authorized a Soviet space plane. The Soviets poured over $10 billion into its development and construction, and came up with a system that used the *Buran* ("blizzard") space plane and the *Energia* ("energy") launcher.

Buran had four turbojets on the space plane, used both for vertical takeoff and landing. *Energia* used four LO_2-kerosene strap-on boosters, and a central core fueled with liquid hydrogen and liquid oxygen.

Five *Buran* Orbiters were planned, but only one was completed which launched once. This *Buran* was a test item with no life support system or computer displays installed. When it flew for the first time on

November 15, 1988, it was launched, unmanned, with no payload, and successfully landed with automated robotics.

The second *Buran* was scheduled for a manned mission in 1993. It was nearing completion when the Soviet Union collapsed in 1991. By then it was obvious that the American Shuttle was not a military system. Lacking a purpose, the Russian program was suspended, then canceled.

The European Space Agency (ESA) also planned a space plane. *Hermes* started as a French initiative. They planned a space plane carrying four to six astronauts and a payload of 4,500kg (around 10,000lb) to low-Earth orbit, atop an Ariane 5 booster. Its first flight was scheduled for 1995.

The French space agency, CNES, initiated *Hermes* in 1984. In 1987 *Hermes* was transferred to the ESA, and as the design progressed, the weight and cost of the vehicle grew dramatically. Development was initially priced in 1984 at $2 billion US dollars. By 1991, *Hermes* had consumed $2 billion, and was expected to eat another $11 billion before its first launch – which was scheduled for 2002. A downsized *Hermes* was considered, but ESA canceled the project in 1992.

American attempts to replace or significantly upgrade the Shuttle were similarly barren. The first attempt came during shuttle development. The Shuttle-C was a heavy-lift variant. Using the same SRBs and ET, the Shuttle-C substituted a wingless, unmanned "can" for the Orbiter. In some versions the SSME section, OMS/RCS pods, and flight control systems were detachable modules retrievable by the Orbiter for reuse. Although the Shuttle-C would have proved a valuable supplement to the Orbiter, it never got beyond the planning phase.

Two other space planes were proposed following *Challenger*. The X-30 National Aerospace Plane (NASP) was a possible Shuttle replacement. A single-stage-to-orbit space plane, which used scramjets that converted to rockets for propulsion, the program was started in 1990. It was canceled while in the design phase. The X-38 (Crew Emergency Reentry Vehicle) was intended as a space-going lifeboat. Carried aboard the Orbiter, it would be docked on the International Space Station (ISS), where it could return the crew to Earth in an emergency. CERV progressed to the prototype stage, with drop tests conducted from a B-52, before cancellation in 1998.

ABOVE ***Hermes* was the ESA's attempt to design a manned orbital space plane. The only thing that took off in this project was cost – which led to its cancellation. (Courtesy ESA)**

LEFT **The X-38, Crew Emergency Reentry Vehicle, was one of the proposed Shuttle successors. This captures the CERV during a drop test prior to cancellation of the program in 1998.**

OPERATIONAL HISTORY

Approach and landing tests

NASA prefers unmanned testing of manned systems before flying a crew, but the Shuttle lacked an unmanned capability. For safety, some systems require human intervention. The crew aboard the Orbiter pulls a lever to lower the landing gear, for example, and the Orbiter lacked a crew escape system. There were two ejection seats installed on *Enterprise* and *Columbia*, but these were to be removed once the Shuttle was declared operational.

NASA planned an unprecedented level of testing prior to the first manned flight, including the Approach and Landing Tests (ALT). Five drop flights were planned. Before flying the drop missions, NASA conducted background testing. Initially, *Enterprise* was mounted atop the 747 and several taxi tests were made to check the structural and dynamic integrity of the odd coupling. A tail cone was added to *Enterprise* to reduce aerodynamic turbulence.

The Orbiter first flew on February 18, 1977. The vehicle was unmanned as it was a captive flight atop a 747 carrier aircraft and was the first of eight such flights. Five captive flights used an unmanned Orbiter. A two-man crew rode in *Enterprise* during the final three captive flights, which were dress rehearsals for the drop tests. The Orbiter's control system were tested, as well as low- and high-speed flutter tests checking the interaction between the 747 and Orbiter. The final captive test flew a separation trajectory.

On August 12, 1977, *Enterprise* was released from the 747, gliding to the dry lakebed runway at Edwards AFB. Four drop flights followed. The boat tail fairing used on the first three flights was removed on the fourth flight. On the fifth flight, November 26, 1977, *Enterprise* landed on a concrete runway, simulating a return from space.

Following ALT, NASA began planning a flight program. Initially, the Shuttle was scheduled to fly in 1979. The planned flight research and development missions belatedly started in 1981, but one early operational Shuttle mission was canceled.

Skylab, America's first space station, was launched in 1973. It lacked an engine, and NASA planned a reboost mission using the Shuttle to carry a

Enterprise separates from the 747 carrier aircraft on the fifth and final ALT flight. This was one of two ALT flights made without the aerodynamic boat tail fairing on the Orbiter, and the only free-flight to land on a concrete runway.

propulsion module to Skylab. This mission was abandoned when Skylab reentered the Earth's atmosphere in July 1979 – four years earlier than expected, and two years before the first Shuttle flight.

A SRB recovered at sea following the STS-1 launch is towed back to KSC by the recovery ship *Liberty*. NASA has two SRB recovery ships, *Liberty* and *Freedom*.

Research and development flights

On April 12, 1981, the Space Shuttle, with Orbiter *Columbia*, entered space. John Young, an astronaut who first flew in Gemini and one of 12 men to have walked on the Moon, commanded the flight. His pilot was Robert Crippen, one of seven former "blue," or military, astronauts transferred to NASA in 1969 when MOL was canceled.

Three other "Research and Development" flights followed STS-1. All had two-man crews, as *Columbia* had only two ejection seats. The commanders were veterans of space – typically having last flown on Apollo missions. The exception, Joe Engle, who commanded STS-2, was an X-15 veteran and flew several ALT missions. The pilots were all former MOL (Manned Orbiting Laboratory) astronauts. Until the *Challenger* accident halted flights, the MOL astronauts proved the backbone of the Shuttle program. They provided the pilots for the first six flights and commanded ten of the next 19 missions.

The focus for the R&D phase was testing the Shuttle. All flights carried instruments to measure Orbiter performance in space. The last three R&D flights tested the Shuttle's Remote Manipulator System (RMS), the "robot arm" that was a fixture on future Shuttle missions. These flights also carried attached payloads on pallets, although none required significant crew attention. On STS-4, one of the pallets was a secret Department of Defense payload, carried along with the otherwise unclassified mix of experiments.

Even as Shuttle carried its first military payload, the Air Force was having second thoughts. The program was late and early predictions about its reusability were wildly optimistic. Flying a virtually empty Orbiter, with minimal payload processing, the Shuttle flew only three times in its first year of flights. Congress mandated that the Shuttle would be the United States' only launch vehicle. A backlog of satellites intended for Shuttle launch had accumulated – and worse, the Defense Department would have to compete for Shuttle launch slots.

The military hedged its Shuttle bet, placing orders for expendable launchers long after the time that they initially agreed to stop using them. National security and slips in the Shuttle program justified this supposedly stopgap action.

STS-4 underscored the difficulty of maintaining security within an essentially civilian program. Operational security requires non-sensitive activities to be kept secret, lest those details allow an analyst to determine secrets. (Payloads described in "Military Missions" were determined in that manner.)

Johnson Space Center (JSC), where the missions were planned and developed, was then an open facility visited by hundreds of tourists daily. The secure facility for Shuttle software was in Building 30, the site of JSC's Mission Control Center, one of the Center's most popular tourist attractions. Yet the Air Force could not afford to build a parallel facility in a secure location because their Shuttle budget was being consumed by the construction of SLC-6.

Following STS-4 the Shuttle was declared "operational." The Shuttle remained a developmental and experimental vehicle, but NASA had sold the system as a space "airliner," so despite those realities the operational era began.

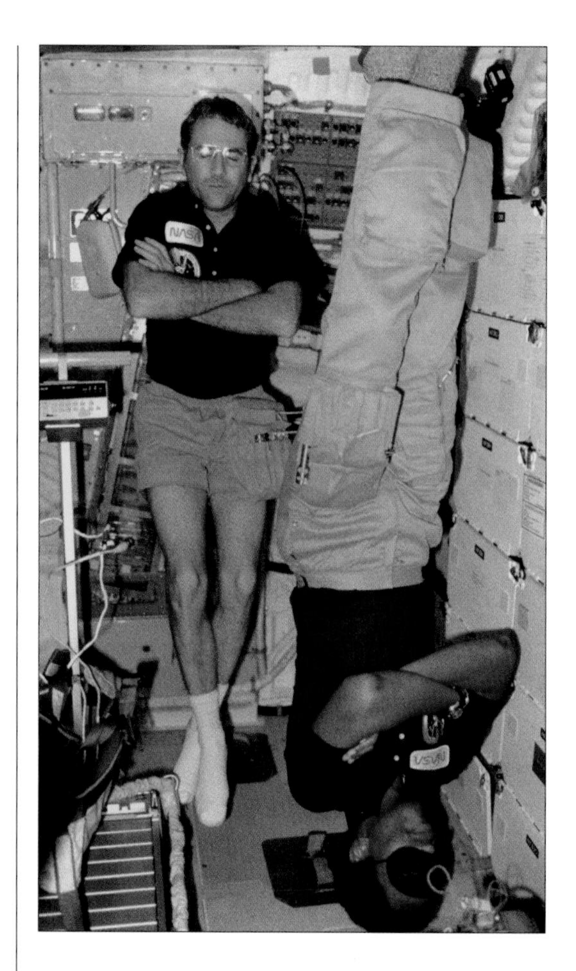

Life aboard the Orbiter. Dick Truly (back) and Guion Bluford (forward) sleeping in the Shuttle middeck. In a weightless environment, up and down are relative concepts.

OPPOSITE, TOP ***Challenger*, captured in orbit by a camera aboard the SPAS free-flyer during STS-7. SPAS, deployed with the RMS (forming a "7" in the front of the payload bay), became the first free-flyer successfully flown from the Orbiter. The two white structures in the aft of the payload bay are cradles for PAM satellites which were also deployed during the mission.**

OPPOSITE, BOTTOM **A standard Shuttle mission in the operational era saw the Orbiter deploy a satellite to a transfer orbit, where a solid fuel upper stage would loft it to its final orbit. Most military Shuttle missions followed this profile.**

The operational era

With STS-5, the Shuttle opened for business. In practice this meant that crew size was increased, the ejection seats were disabled, and the Orbiters began deploying satellites.

The first two operational flights demonstrated the program's immaturity. For the first time the PAM (Payload Assist Module) or IUS (Inertial Upper Stage) were used to send satellites to geostationary orbit. Two communications satellites deployed on STS-5 and a critical Tracking and Data Relay System Satellite (TDRSS) deployed on STS-6 went astray following upper stage failures. Additionally, the first Shuttle-era spacewalk, scheduled for STS-5, was canceled when the spacesuit malfunctioned. It was instead conducted on STS-6.

These problems were typical of those seen in the initial phases of every program pushing technological limits. All were quickly fixed, and not repeated. NASA recovered and refurbished the two communications satellites lost on STS-5, and circularized TDRSS in a usable orbit. In retrospect, the surprise was that there were so few failures, and those that occurred were relatively minor.

For 19 missions, from STS-7 to the final flight of *Challenger* on Mission 51-L, the Shuttle seemed about to deliver on the extravagant promise made for it. It served as a platform to rescue and repair satellites – starting with the Solar Max on 41-C. It provided a "shirtsleeve" environment for space travelers. It transported the ESA Spacelab module – a manned laboratory that fit in the cargo bay – on two missions. It carried as many as eight people into space in one mission.

Columbia was joined by *Challenger*, then *Discovery* and *Atlantis*. Lightweight ETs became available, and lightweight filament-wound SRBs were on track for a first Vandenberg launch in July 1986. The second crawler came on-line in 1983. The second launch pad – allowing two launches in one month – was ready in January 1986.

The "operational" era was illusory. There were nine launches in 1985, but only through massive effort. Personnel worked overtime. Equipment was shuffled from one Shuttle to another. Margins were shaved. Missions slipped, were canceled, or reshuffled.

The techno-thriller era of military space never occurred. By 1980, military space was the province of robots. Both the US and USSR orbited unmanned satellites to watch and monitor the activities of their foes, or relay the information captured by other satellites.

The Air Force was using the Shuttle as a simple delivery system. For routine satellite launches Shuttle was less capable, flexible, and reliable than expendables and more expensive. Additionally, launching military satellites to geostationary orbits was routine and unremarkable when launched from expendable boosters. The Air Force saw that a manned launch vehicle turned every military mission into a media circus, with the press speculating wildly about the mission. The press "knew" the Air Force would not use the Shuttle for routine satellite launches – although this is exactly what the Air Force did use it for.

NASA abandoned the "STS" numbering system in 1983 replacing the sequential numbering with a coded collection of numbers and letters. Officially the change was done to identify the launch site – Vandenberg or Kennedy. Unofficially, many believed that the new system was to disguise launch manifest changes caused when problems occurred.

1986 was to have been the year that the Shuttle proved itself. Fifteen missions were planned, including the two Vandenberg launches, and two missions, 61-F and 61-G, scheduled to launch interplanetary probes that used Centaur upper stages.

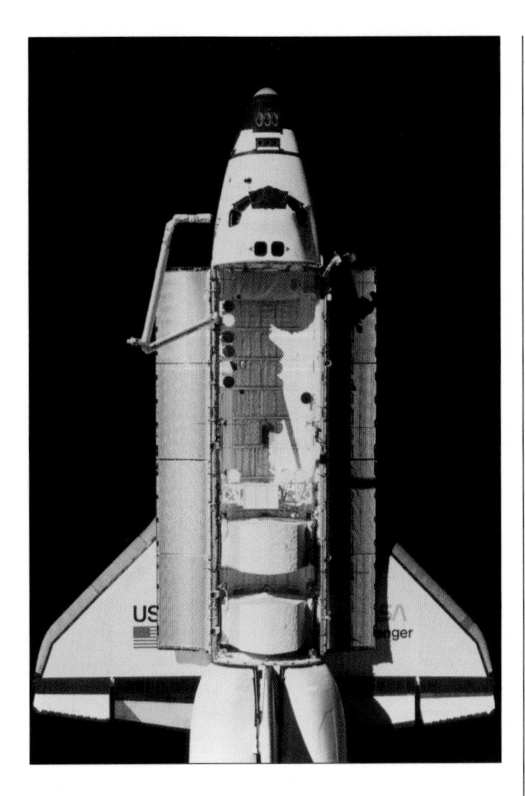

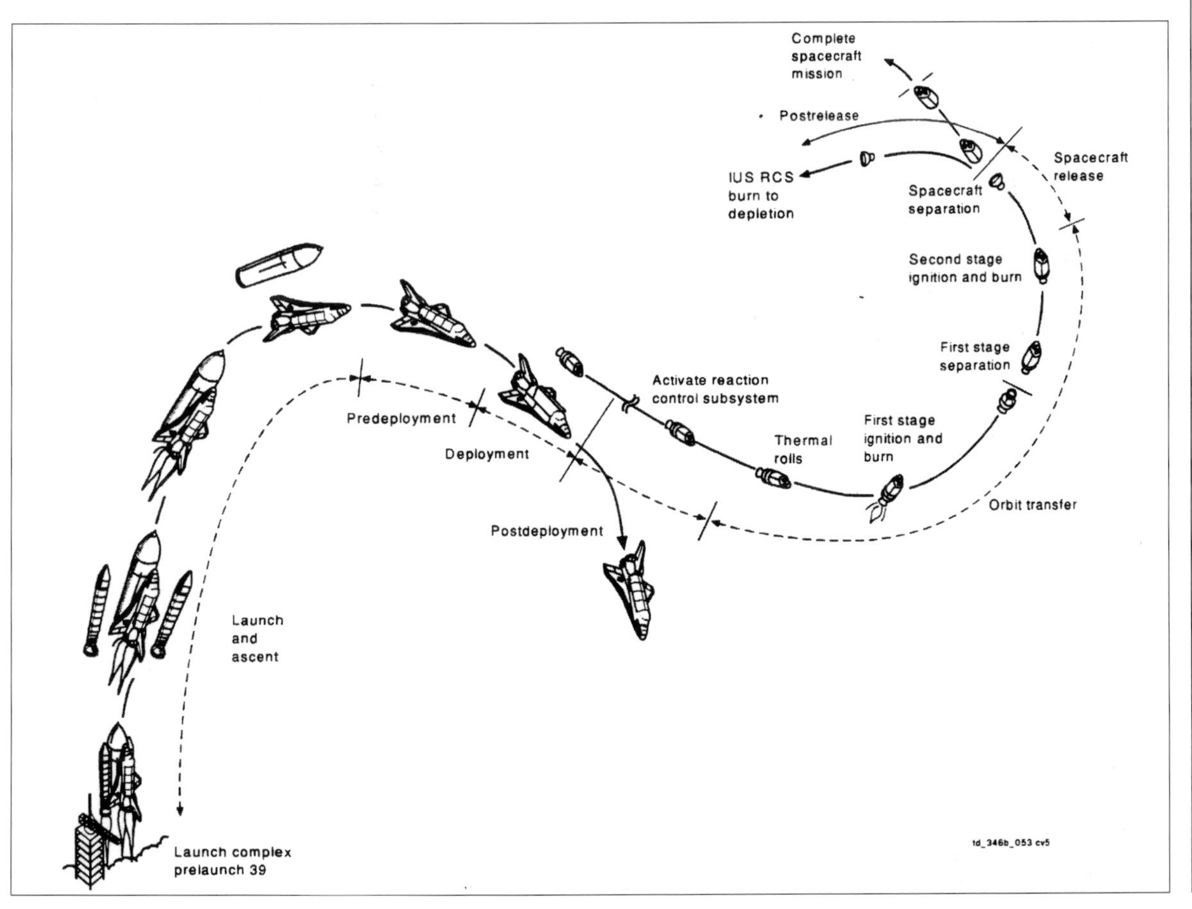

***Challenger* was lost following liftoff of the 25th Shuttle mission. Here, one of the SRBs can be seen flying out of the cloud shrouding the disintegration of the External Tank. Range safety destroyed the SRB shortly after a tracking camera captured this image.**

All four missions were at the edge of the Shuttle's performance ability. All required the SSME to run at 109% of rated power – a jump from the 104% used on standard missions. All had virtually no abort to orbit capability – the ability to put the Orbiter into a lower orbit than planned, so that Mission Control could evaluate options. Instead, if the engines faltered, the Orbiter had to conduct a riskier Abort Once Around (AOA) landing after one revolution, in some cases with a liquid-fueled payload still aboard.

Many flight controllers expected problems on those flights. Instead, trouble came unexpectedly in January, 1986. 51-L began as a routine TDRSS deployment with a schoolteacher as part of *Challenger*'s flight crew. The Shuttle disintegrated 71 seconds after launch.

Return to flight and beyond

The *Challenger* accident forced reevaluation of the Shuttle. Investigations revealed a design flaw – an SRB field joint linking two SRB segments allowed hot gasses to escape the SRB during cold weather. These leaks occurred on several other flights. On the fatal *Challenger* mission, the leak was on the inboard side of the SRB. It cut the strut separating the SRB from the External Tank (ET), allowing the SRB to swing and rupture the ET.

The investigation also revealed serious management problems in NASA. Rather than demonstrating that the Shuttle was safe to fly before proceeding with the launch, on 51-L engineers had to prove that the Shuttle was unsafe to fly to stop the launch. This violated flight rules, but the pressure to keep the Shuttle "operational" had shifted NASA's priorities. The main cause of launch schedule pressure was less the mission scheduled for 51-L (even with the high-visibility "Teacher in Space" aboard). Rather, 51-L had to launch in January so *Challenger* could be prepared for an inflexible interplanetary launch in May 1986.

The physical problems were fixed. The joint was redesigned, and the SRBs are now probably the safest part of the system. Several other minor changes were made to the Shuttle. There was no similar overhaul of NASA's management.

Challenger did force a realistic reappraisal of the Shuttle's capabilities. NASA finally admitted that the Shuttle was uneconomical as a launch system for commercial satellites. Only TDRSS and Orbiter-tended satellites, such as the Hubble Space Telescope (an orbiting optical telescope), would be launched using the Shuttle. The Centaur was deleted as a Shuttle upper stage, as it was too dangerous. Satellites already manifested for the Orbiter would be launched from the Shuttle. New satellites would be launched on expendables. The Shuttle would now focus on science missions.

The Air Force pulled the plug on their involvement with the Shuttle following *Challenger*. The *Challenger* hiatus delayed deployment of several critical satellites, making it difficult to monitor the Soviet Union during a critical phase of what proved to be the first steps of its disintegration. SLC-6 was incomplete in early 1986 and these deficiencies required expensive rework. Post-*Challenger* modifications reduced the Shuttle's payload, rendering it incapable of lofting critical military payloads into a polar orbit from SLC-6. The Shuttle lacked operational flexibility – the Air Force could not quickly schedule a Shuttle mission to respond to a national crisis.

The military decided to use the Shuttle to launch any already-completed satellites originally manifested for the Shuttle. Others would be converted so they could be launched on expendables. Between 1988 and 1992 eight military flights were conducted. Six flights launched satellites. Two others used free-flyers deployed from and retrieved by the Orbiter in military research missions. The last DOD missions, overtaken by the collapse of the Soviet Union, carried unclassified payloads in addition to their military cargo.

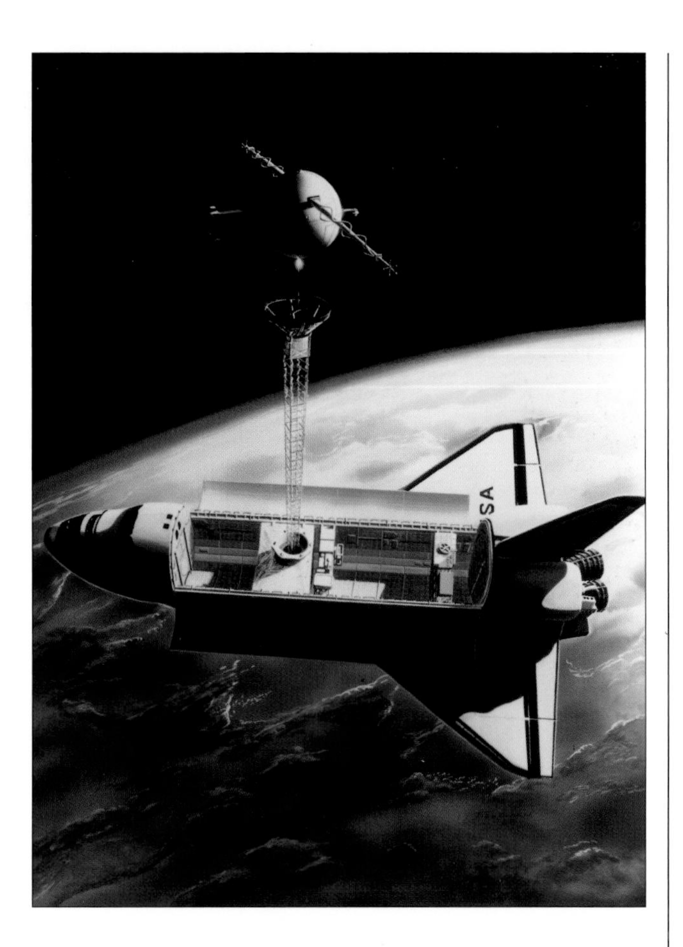

An artist's concept of the Tether Satellite System deployment. An ambitious project, TSS was flown twice on the Orbiter. Neither mission was successful. In the first mission the TSS jammed after reeling out a few hundred feet. In the second mission, the tether broke when the TSS was fully deployed, 20km (12.5 miles) from the Orbiter.

The first flight after *Challenger*, STS-26, returned to the old numbering system, as if announcing the end of the operational era. It carried a replacement for the TDRSS lost on 51-L. Interplanetary probes scheduled for Centaur missions were launched with an IUS upper stage. STS-30 carried the *Magellan* probe which was sent to Venus, and STS-34 launched *Galileo* to Jupiter. Since the IUS had less thrust than the Centaur, *Galileo* used gravitational assists from Venus, then Earth, to reach Jupiter. STS-32, in January 1990, retrieved the Long Duration Exposure Facility – placed in orbit by *Challenger*, but stranded by the launch hiatus – literally months before it would have reentered the atmosphere.

This period also saw several other pioneering missions, including the deployment of the Hubble Space Telescope and Compton (Infrared telescope) observatories, and two tethered satellite missions, where the Orbiter reeled a subsatellite out on a 20km(12.5 mile) tether.

International Space Station

Beginning in the early 1990s the Shuttle gained a new mission, building an orbital space station, and thus returned to NASA's original intention for the vehicle. As with the development of the Shuttle, the development of the space station was neither straightforward, nor untroubled. Announced as an objective by President Reagan after *Challenger*, in its original incarnation, the space station was solely a United States affair, Space Station *Freedom*. Eventually, *Freedom* included participation from ESA, NASDA (the Japanese space agency), and the Soviets.

ABOVE ***Atlantis* departure from *Mir* in 1996. This photo, taken from a Soyuz TM, as it approached *Mir*, is a rare side view of the Orbiter in space. Normally the Orbiter approaches other orbital vehicles with the payload bay facing the target.**

In 1992 *Freedom* was suspended in favor of a new design. The primary feature of the new plan was greater Russian participation. Following the collapse of the Soviet Union in 1991, the Russian space agency lost most of its funding. A partnership with the United States was one way to maintain a Russian space capability. While the USA had backed away from orbital space stations following *Skylab* in 1973, Russia launched a series of *Salyut* and *Mir* space stations throughout a 30-year period. Long-duration on-orbit experience was one area where the Russians outperformed the United States in space, and both gained from the partnership.

Initially, starting in the middle 1990s, Shuttle participation in the space station program consisted of trips to the Russian *Mir* space station. These were advertised as a way of familiarizing both nations with the processes of the other. In reality, the first elements of the new space station – called the International Space Station (ISS) – would not be ready until 1998. Both nations wanted a mission for their manned space programs until ISS was ready for assembly. While some benefits were gained by the nine Shuttle visits to *Mir*, these flights preserved *Mir* past its service life.

Finally, in February 1998, STS-88 delivered the first of nearly 50 packages that would constitute the ISS. Of the 19 Shuttle missions since STS-88, 14 have been devoted to the ISS. The most recent flew in November 2002. Virtually all of the scheduled future Shuttle missions,

RIGHT **All that remains. Recovered debris from *Columbia* in a hangar at KSC. Following the loss of *Columbia* in February 2003, NASA scoured the Texas countryside for pieces of the Orbiter as part of the effort to determine what caused the breakup.**

with the exception of the final Hubble Space Telescope servicing mission, go to ISS.

The loss of *Columbia* in 2002 during STS-107 – a stand-alone Spacelab mission – may accelerate the exclusive use of the Shuttle for ISS missions. The Orbiter was lost after the Thermal Protection System (TPS) was damaged during liftoff. A tile inspection system will fly on all future missions, but on ISS missions ISS can serve as a "lifeboat" for the Orbiter's crew until either the TPS is repaired or a rescue mission can be launched.

Regardless of the future, the Shuttle has a remarkable record. Conceived during the Cold War as an Apollo follow-on, it may be remembered more for what it failed to accomplish rather than for its real achievements. If it failed as a space bus and an orbital warplane, it has carried more humans into space than any other launch system. It remains the world's only reusable space system.

Military missions

Ten military missions were flown on the Space Shuttle. Four other military missions planned for Kennedy launch were canceled, either due to payload problems or following the *Challenger* disaster. Seven polar missions were planned using the Vandenberg launch site. All were scheduled after January 1986, and canceled after *Challenger*; only two were under active development before cancellation.

Flown Military Missions

51-C
Vehicle: *Discovery*
Orbit: 28.5° inclination, 220nmi altitude
Crew: 5
Launch: January 24, 1985, Pad 39-A
Landing: January 27, 1985, KSC Runway 15

Mission patches for the ten Department of Defense Shuttle flights. From left to right: Top row: 51-C, 51-J, STS-27. Middle row: STS-28, STS-33, STS-36, STS-38. Bottom row: STS-39, STS-44, STS-53.

The first dedicated military mission, 51-C carried a classified cargo: a Magnum model geostationary electronic intelligence satellite. The mission – a routine delivery of a satellite to orbit using an IUS upper stage – highlighted the problem of military use of the Orbiter. A satellite that could have been quietly launched on an expendable was launched with the publicity that attended every NASA manned launch.

51-J
Vehicle: *Atlantis*
Orbit: 28.5° inclination, 319nmi altitude
Crew: 5
Launch: October 3, 1985, Pad 39-A
Landing: October 7, 1985, Edwards AFB Runway 23
The first launch of the Orbiter *Atlantis*, this second Defense Department mission deployed two DSCS-III military communications satellites for the United States Air Force, using a single IUS to boost both to geostationary orbits.

STS-27
Vehicle: *Atlantis*
Orbit: 57° inclination, 220nmi altitude
Crew: 5
Launch: December 2, 1988, Pad 39-B
Landing: December 6, 1988, Edwards AFB Runway 17
The first military mission following *Challenger*, STS-27 deployed a Lacrosse reconnaissance satellite. Lacrosse uses side-looking radar for an all-weather capability. It does not have a booster stage. This Lacrosse placed into orbit by *Atlantis* was the lowest of four Lacrosse satellites.

STS-28
Vehicle: *Columbia*
Orbit: 57° inclination, 166nmi altitude
Crew: 5
Launch: August 8, 1989, Pad 39-B
Landing: August 13, 1989, Edwards AFB Runway 17
STS-28 deployed a subsatellite ferret (SSF) and SDS-2 communications satellite. The SSF is believed to be a one-off design, produced to test the COBRA BRASS imaging system currently used for optical reconnaissance. SDS-2 is a high-inclination communications satellite in a highly elliptical "Molniya" orbit used to relay secure communications from other military satellites to prevent interception.

STS-33
Vehicle: *Discovery*
Orbit: 28.5° inclination, 302nmi altitude
Crew: 5
Launch: November 22, 1989, Pad 39-B
Landing: November 27, 1989, Edwards AFB Runway 4
STS-33 deployed the second Magnum model geostationary electronic intelligence satellite. Once deployed, it was boosted into a geostationary orbit by an IUS upper stage. This mission was a night launch, the first DoD night launch and the third program night launch.

A night launch of the Shuttle, as seen from the Shuttle Training Aircraft as it flew near the pad. This image captures the launch of STS-33, one of the ten military Shuttle missions.

STS-36
Vehicle: *Atlantis*
Orbit: 62° inclination, 132nmi altitude
Crew: 5
Launch: February 28, 1990, Pad 39-A
Landing: March 4, 1990, Edwards AFB Runway 23
The mission for which the Shuttle had been designed: STS-36 deployed the KH-12 reconnaissance satellite. This payload had defined the size of the cargo bay, and the maximum capacity of the Orbiter. The satellite was intended for a sun-synchronous orbit (97.7° inclination), possible only when launched from Vandenberg. Subsequent KH-12s were redesigned for launch from Titan-4s, although the first KH-12 was nearly complete when this decision was made. Combined with the age of then-available KH-11 satellites, this KH-12 was deployed at a sub-optimal inclination. Even with a 62°-inclination launch, the Orbiter was at the edge of its performance limits in placing this 43,130lb (19,600kg) payload in orbit.

STS-38
Vehicle: *Atlantis*
Orbit: 28.5° inclination, 142nmi altitude
Crew: 5
Launch November 15, 1990, Pad 39-A
Landing: November 20, 1990, KSC Runway 33
The third launch of a Magnum model geostationary electronic intelligence satellite.

STS-39
Vehicle: *Discovery*
Orbit: 57° inclination, 140nmi altitude
Crew: 5
Launch April 28, 1991, Pad 39-A
Landing: May 6, 1991, KSC Runway 15

A dedicated Department of Defense mission, STS-39 contained mostly unclassified payloads. These included Air Force Program-675 (AFP675); Infrared Background Signature Survey (IBSS) with Critical Ionization Velocity (CIV), Chemical Release Observation (CRO) and Shuttle Pallet Satellite-II (SPAS-II) experiments; and Space Test Payload-1 (STP-1). Classified payloads consisted of Multi-Purpose Release Canister (MPEC). Also aboard was Radiation Monitoring Equipment III (RME III) and Cloud Logic to Optimize Use of Defense Systems-IA (CLOUDS-I).

STS-44
Vehicle:*Discovery*
Orbit: 28.5° inclination, 197nmi altitude
Crew: 5
Launch: November 24, 1991, Pad 39-A
Landing: December 1, 1991, Edwards AFB Runway 5
Another dedicated Department of Defense mission with unclassified payloads. The Orbiter deployed a Defense Support Program (DSP) satellite, an early-warning satellite. It was boosted into a geosynchronous orbit with an IUS. It also carried numerous cargo bay and middeck payloads.

STS-53
Vehicle: *Discovery*
Orbit: 57° inclination, 174nmi altitude
Crew: 5
Launch: December 2, 1992, Pad 39-A
Landing: December 9, 1992, Edwards AFB Runway 22
The final military mission deployed another SDS-2 satellite, USA 89. Secondary payloads in the cargo bay included the Orbital Debris Radar Calibration Spheres (ODERACS) and the combined Shuttle Glow Experiment/Cryogenic Heat Pipe Experiment (GCP).

Columbia **at Edwards AFB being towed to the Shuttle Processing Area at NASA's Dryden Flight Research Center following landing on STS-5. Orbiter landing servicing vehicles can be seen behind the Orbiter, while a tug pulls the Orbiter.**

A: Profiles of Orbiters

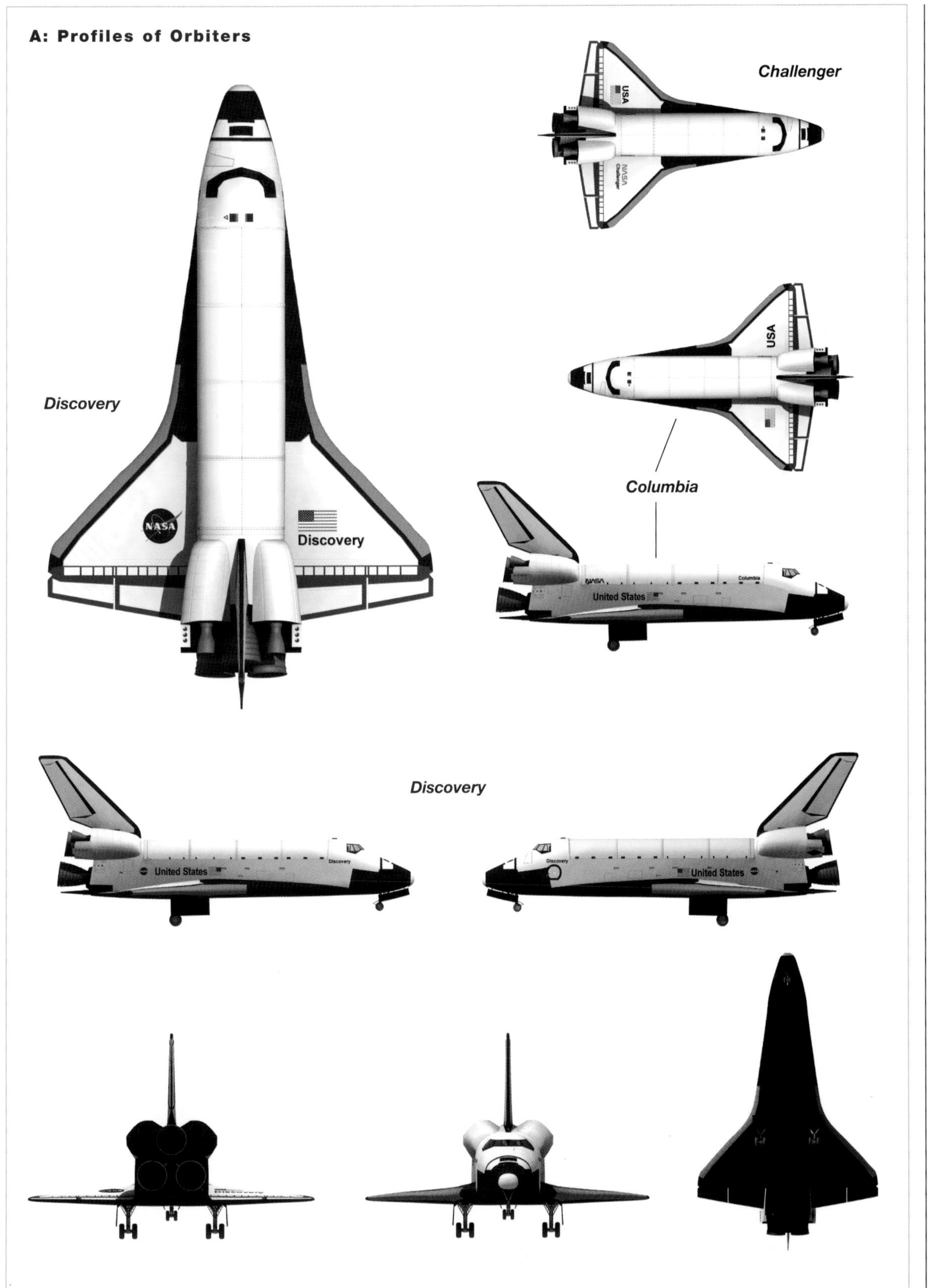

B: STS-1 launch

C: Flight deck/cockpit
1
2

D: CUTAWAY OF SHUTTLE STACK

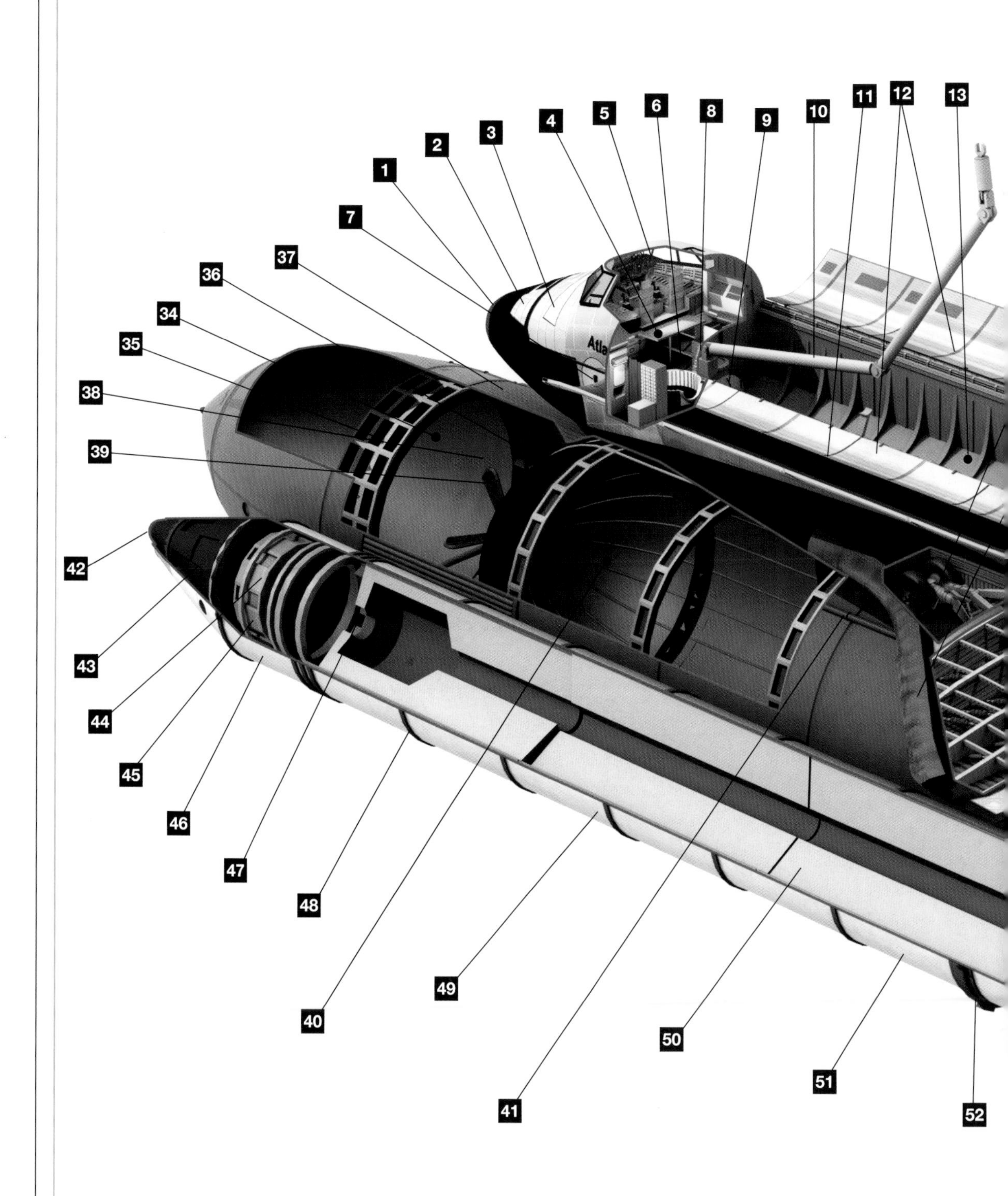

KEY

1 Reinforced Carbon-Carbon (RCC) nose
2 Forward Reaction Control System
3 Star tracker
4 Crew module
5 Flight deck
6 Mid-deck
7 Hatch
8 Mid-deck lockers
9 Airlock
10 RMS
11 Payload bay doors
12 Radiators
13 Payload bay
14 Main landing gear
15 Leading edge RCC
16 OMS pod
17 RCS monomethyl hydrazine tank
18 RCS nitrogen tetroxide tank
19 OMS monomethyl hydrazine tank
20 OMS nitrogen tetroxide tank
21 Auxiliary power unit
22 Rudder
23 Speed brake
24 Aft RCS unit
25 OMS engine
26 Primary RCS thruster
27 Vernier RCS thruster
28 Liquid oxygen fuel line
29 Liquid hydrogen fuel line
30 Main engine bell
31 Outer elevon
32 Inner elevon
33 Body flap

External tank

34 Liquid oxygen tank
35 Forward slosh baffle
36 Intertank
37 Thrust panel
38 SRB beam
39 Anti-vortex baffles
40 Liquid hydrogen tank
41 Fuel lines

Solid rocket boosters

42 Nose cap with drogue chute
43 Frustrum with three main parachutes
44 Camera pod
45 Avionics
46 Forward skirt
47 Igniter
48 Forward segment
49 Forward mid segment
50 Solid propellant
51 Aft mid segment
52 Attach ring
53 Aft segment (with nozzle)
54 Aft skirt
55 Booster holddown posts (4)
56 Nozzle extension

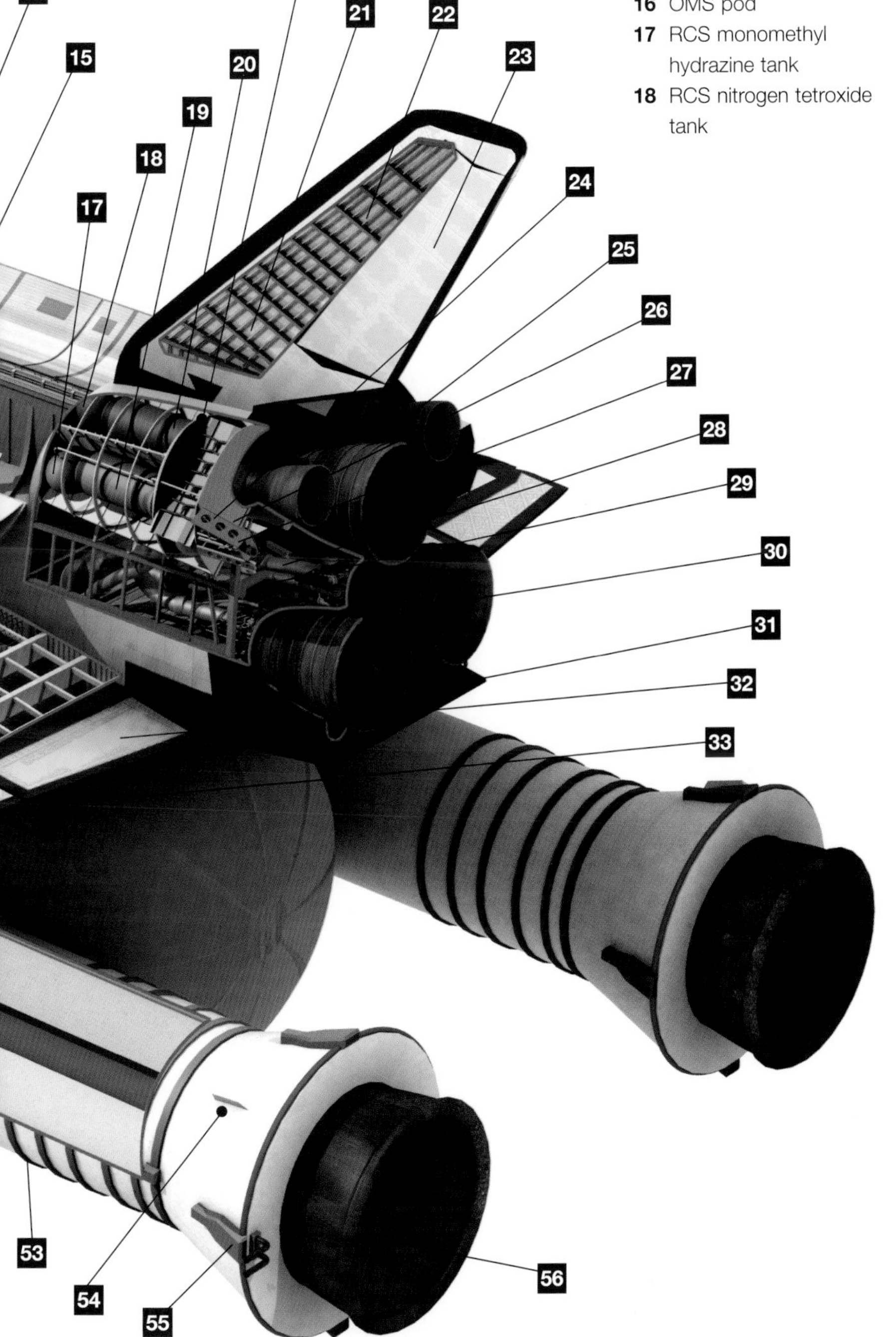

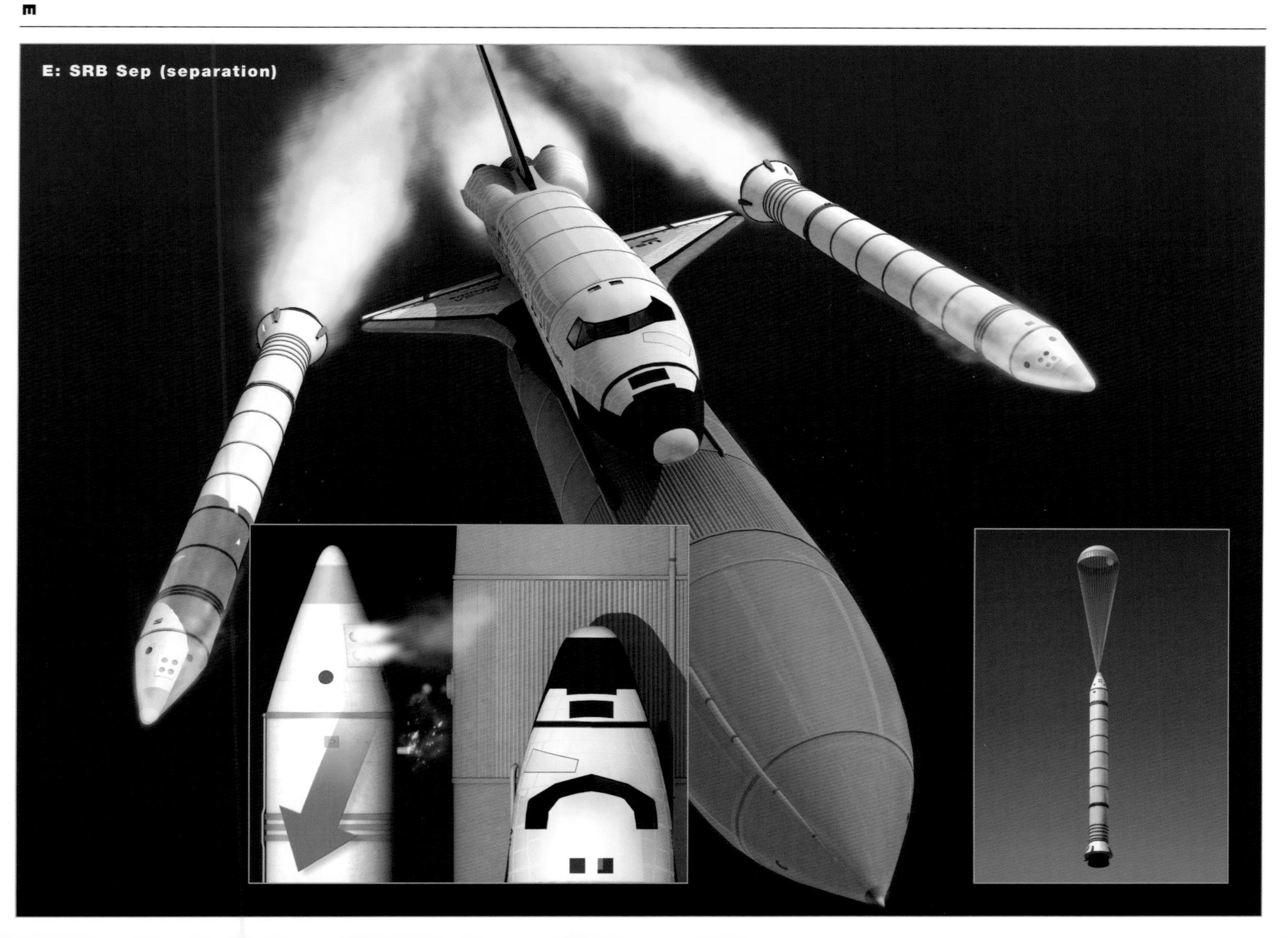

E: SRB Sep (separation)

F: Landing

G: HST repair

The mission that never was. The crew of 62-A, the first planned Vandenberg flight, poses for its official mission photo. In the background, the never-used SLC-6 launch complex can be seen. The Orbiter is probably *Enterprise*, used for SLC-6 fit tests.

Mid-deck experiments included Microcapsules in Space (MIS-l); Space Tissue Loss (STL); Visual Function Tester (VFT-2); Cosmic Radiation Effects and Activation Monitor (CREAM); Radiation Monitoring Equipment (RME-III); Fluid Acquisition and Resupply Experiment (FARE); Hand-held, Earth-oriented, Real-time, Cooperative, User-friendly, Location-targeting and Environmental System (HERCULES); Battlefield Laser Acquisition Sensor Test (BLAST); and the Cloud Logic to Optimize Use of Defense Systems (CLOUDS).

Cancelled Military Missions

STS-10 and 41-E, and 41-H

These were military flights originally scheduled for 1984 and 1985, which were canceled due to IUS development problems and left the Air Force with no means of launching scheduled payloads in orbit. It is likely that the payloads flown in the first four Defense Department missions were originally intended for these flights.

62-A, 62-B

These were the first of nearly a dozen launches scheduled from Vandenberg Air Force Base, using the SLC-6 complex. They may be the only two that reached the planning stage. 62-A was scheduled for July 1986, and 62-B for late September. 62-A had a crew of six commanded by Robert Crippen (the pilot on STS-1). The mission would probably have launched a TEAL RUBY sensor test satellite, with the first KH-12 being lofted in 62-B in September. Problems with SLC-6 probably caused both of these missions to slip and they were abandoned completely following *Challenger* when SLC-6 was abandoned, and all Vandenberg flights scrubbed.

61-N

A KSC DOD mission scheduled for September 1986, it was canceled following *Challenger*. It would probably have carried one of the cargoes launched in STS-27 or STS-28.

ORBITER VEHICLES

OV-101 *Enterprise*

The first Shuttle Orbiter, OV-101 was originally to have been named *Constitution*, to celebrate the American bicentennial and to honor "Old Ironside," the sailing frigate *Constitution*. The name was changed when fans of the science fiction show *Star Trek* petitioned to change the name to *Enterprise*, the starship in the TV show. President Gerald Ford had served in the US Navy in the Pacific during World War II, and it is likely that he viewed the name change as honoring another notable *Enterprise*, the aircraft carrier CV-6, which fought through the war.

Enterprise was rolled out on September 17, 1976, at Rockwell International's Palmdale assembly plant. On January 31, 1977, it was towed overland 36 miles to the Dryden Flight Research Center in California, where it was used in the Approach and Landing Tests.

Enterprise flew 17 times during the nine-month ALT program. It initially flew five unmanned captive flights atop a 747 carrier aircraft, testing structural integrity and handling characteristics. This was followed by three manned captive flights with a two-man crew in the Orbiter to test the flight control system before the drop tests. This included a dress rehearsal for the drop tests.

Five more flights ensued when *Enterprise* was released from the 747 and glided to a landing at Edwards Air Force Base, adjacent to Dryden. These tests verified that the Orbiter would perform as expected during reentry. On the final two free-flight tests, the tail cone (known as a boat tail), normally used when the Orbiter was carried by the 747 to reduce turbulence, was removed. The Orbiter was dropped with three simulated SSME engine bells and two simulated OMS engine bells to test its performance when these were aerodynamically exposed. The final drop test simulated a return from space, as closely as possible, with *Enterprise* landing on the concrete runway, instead of the dry lake bed as had been done for the other tests. The final four ALT flights tested ferrying the Orbiter with the 747.

Following the ALT flights, *Enterprise* was flown to Marshall Space Flight Center in Alabama, arriving on March 13, 1978. Mated with an External Tank and two Solid Rocket Boosters, it spent the next year in vertical vibration tests.

On April 10, 1979, *Enterprise* was ferried to the Kennedy Space Center, mated with an ET and two SRBs, and used in a series of fit tests involving the refurbished Pad 39-A. This also enabled ground crews to practice launch preparation procedures.

Transferred back to Dryden on August 16, 1979, *Enterprise* was returned to Palmdale. Initial plans had called for *Enterprise* to be converted to space flight status, and follow *Columbia* into space. Partly as a result of *Enterprise*'s tests, the design of the Orbiter had evolved, and while similar in appearance, *Columbia* and its sisters incorporated significant structural and internal improvements. Due to the cost of retrofitting *Enterprise* to flight status, NASA decided to convert a test article into a flying Orbiter, and retire *Enterprise*.

Enterprise about to enter the Heading Alignment Circle (HAC) preparatory to landing at Edwards AFB on the third Approach and Landing Test free flight.

Between 1981 and 1984 *Enterprise* was ferried to various fairs and air shows in Europe and North America for publicity purposes. In November 1984 *Enterprise* was taken to Vandenberg AFB, where it was used for fit tests at SLC-6, the intended polar mission launch site. On Nov. 18, 1985, *Enterprise* was flown to Dulles Airport, Washington, D.C., and sent to the Smithsonian Institution for display in the Air and Space Museum. Following the *Columbia* accident, components from *Enterprise* were removed and used in the accident investigation.

OV-102 *Columbia*

The first Orbiter in space, *Columbia* was named after a sloop, *Columbia,* which discovered the Columbia River in 1792. That *Columbia* was also the first ship from the United States to complete a circumnavigation of the world.

Columbia rolled out of the Palmdale Assembly plant on March 8, 1979, and was ferried to KSC later that month. While originally intended to first fly in 1979, lagging development of key systems such as the main engines and thermal protection system kept *Columbia* grounded for the next two years. *Columbia* was used for integrated testing in 1980 and 1981, culminating in a flight readiness firing that certified the SSMEs on March 20, 1981.

Following the first launch, on April 12, 1981 (STS-1), *Columbia* flew the next four missions before being joined by *Challenger.* This included STS-3, the only Shuttle mission to land at White Sands in New Mexico, and STS-5, the first "operational" Shuttle mission, and the first with a crew greater than two, carrying five astronauts, then a record.

Following STS-5, in November 1982, *Columbia* was sent to Palmdale, where the ejection seats for the commander and pilot – used during the flight test missions (STS-1 through 4) – were removed, and the vehicle modified to carry laboratory modules.

Columbia flew two more missions before the *Challenger* hiatus: STS-9, the first Spacelab mission; and 61-C, an extended-duration mission combining satellite deployments with space science research.

Following return to flight, *Columbia* flew another 21 missions. While some were satellite deployments, *Columbia* flew the bulk of the Spacelab and Spacehab missions, missions with a habitable laboratory in the cargo bay. Of the 17 missions using a laboratory module, *Columbia* flew 12, and 11 of the 13 following the *Challenger* hiatus.

One reason for this was, as the heaviest Orbiter, *Columbia* was ill-suited for missions which stretched Shuttle's performance abilities. It could not have been launched from Vandenberg, nor was it ever assigned a payload involving a Centaur or IUS upper stage, and only flew one military mission.

Columbia was initially incapable of reaching the International Space Station (ISS), although a refit in 1999 rectified this, and it was scheduled for a Space Station resupply flight in 2003. Alone of the active Orbiter fleet, *Columbia* was never sent to the ISS. Since the launch of the first ISS element in December 1998, *Columbia* was used for non-ISS missions, including a Hubble Space Telescope servicing mission.

Columbia had three major refits following the 1983 overhaul. In 1991 it went through an overhaul at Palmdale. Fifty changes were made to *Columbia,* including many recommended in the wake of the loss of *Challenger.* These included the addition of a drag chute, carbon brakes,

In space, no one has a good hair day. Astronaut Marsha Ivins wrestles with a thermal imaging camera during the 14-day STS-62 mission. She is near the aft station on the flight deck. The puffy appearance of her face is characteristic of someone in zero gravity over a long period.

enhanced nose-wheel steering, and enhancements to the Thermal Protection System.

In 1994 *Columbia* entered its first Orbiter Maintenance Down Period (OMDP) – a major overhaul and maintenance process. Over 90 modifications and upgrades were made during this process, including improvements to the landing gear thermal barrier and tire pressure monitoring.

In 1999 *Columbia* underwent a second OMDP. The structure was lightened, allowing it to carry a payload to the ISS. *Columbia* became the second Orbiter, after *Atlantis*, to get the new "glass-cockpit" crew displays (see Plate C for a fuller discussion of the glass cockpit).

Columbia was lost on February 1, 2003. The wing leading-edge of the Thermal Protection System (TPS) was damaged during liftoff. On reentry, heating caused the aluminum structure to fail and *Columbia* broke up. The crew of seven, including two women and a guest astronaut from Israel, died.

OV-099 *Challenger*

Challenger was named after HMS *Challenger*, a Royal Navy research vessel that circumnavigated the globe on a scientific expedition during the 1870s. When construction began on what would become *Challenger* in 1975, it was intended as a high-fidelity Structural Test Assembly (STA-099), to be used for stress and vibration testing. Rockwell delivered the completed airframe to Lockheed in February 1978. For 11 months STA-099 underwent testing simulating the stresses and vibrations associated with all mission phases, from liftoff to landing.

As STA-099 was completing testing, NASA realized converting *Enterprise* (OV-101) to flight status would be cost-prohibitive and contracts for follow-on Orbiters had not yet been awarded. Without *Enterprise, Columbia* would be the sole Orbiter until 1983. Since STA-099 was built from flight components, NASA decided to convert it to flight status. A supplemental contract for the conversion was awarded to Rockwell International on January 5, 1979, and Rockwell began construction of the crew cabin – an item originally boilerplated when STA-099 was a test article.

NASA skipped a final round of structural testing that would have damaged the airframe, and STA-099 was returned to Palmdale in November 1979 for conversion to a flight article. Retaining its item number – 099 – it then became Orbital Vehicle 099 or OV-099. The forward fuselage was split and the dummy crew compartment replaced with a new, operational compartment. The wing structure was modified – reinforced and lightened, using the results from the structural testing done on it when it was a test article. The Orbiter that emerged from Palmdale in June 1982 was stronger and 2,900lb lighter than *Columbia.*

Challenger was modified at KSC in 1983. It was one of two Orbiters scheduled to deploy the liquid-fueled Centaur upper stage in spring 1986. Plumbing was added to allow the fuel to be dumped in an abort situation, and controls and instrumentation were added to the aft station to allow the stage to be monitored and controlled.

Challenger's career was brief but spectacular. It achieved several notable program firsts, including:

- The first space walk during the Shuttle program (STS-6)
- Carrying the first American woman in space (STS-7)
- The first free-flying satellite deployed and retrieved during the Shuttle program (SPAS-1, during STS-7),
- First use of the Remote Manipulator System (RMS, during STS-7)
- First night launch and landing (STS-8)
- First untethered spacewalk using the Manned Maneuvering Unit (41-B)
- First KSC landing (41-B)
- Deploying the first satellite to return to orbit (the SPAS pallet flown during STS-7, again flew on 41-B)
- First on-orbit satellite repair (Solar Max, during 41-C)
- Carrying the first woman to walk in space (Katheryn Sullivan, in 41-G)
- First eight-person crew (61-A).

Challenger achieved two less notable firsts. It was the first Orbiter to use an abort launch: 51-F did an abort-to-orbit when one of its SSMEs shut down during the ascent, after a faulty sensor reading. When a second engine was erroneously flagged as running hot *Challenger* nearly became the first Orbiter to do an abort-once-around. The flight controller correctly assessed the problem as a bad sensor, not a bad engine, and overrode the shut-down command. *Challenger* completed the mission from a lower orbit than planned.

Challenger was also the first Orbiter lost. Hot gasses leaking from the SRB melted the strut holding the SRB to the ET. The SRB struck the ET, rupturing the liquid hydrogen tank. Thrown off the stack as the ET collapsed, *Challenger* disintegrated, torn apart by the airflow. All seven crew members aboard died.

OV-103 *Discovery*

The third orbital Orbiter, *Discovery* was named after one of two ships that accompanied the explorer Captain James Cook on his 1776–79 voyage when he discovered the Hawaiian Islands and explored Alaska. The name also honors several other famous ships named *Discovery*, including one sailed by Henry Hudson, and two used by the Royal Geographic Society used to explore the Polar Regions.

Construction began on *Discovery* in 1979, at Rockwell's Palmdale plant. Final assembly was completed on February 25, 1983. Rollout to Dryden following checkout and acceptance testing occurred on October 16, 1983.

Using lessons learned from experience in flying *Columbia* and *Challenger*, *Discovery* and its later sisters were both lighter and stronger than the earlier Orbiters. Many variations are internal, but one visible change involved the Thermal Protection System. Thermal blankets – lighter and easier to maintain than tiles – were substituted on the upper surfaces of the outer wings and forward body. As a result, *Discovery* could carry 6,870lb more payload into orbit than *Columbia.*

Discovery arrived at KSC on November 9, 1983, where it was immediately modified to carry a Centaur liquid-fuel upper stage. *Discovery* went through a nine-month OMDP in 1995–96. A fifth set of cryogenics tanks was added, extending the time it could remain in orbit,

One of the highlights of the Shuttle program occurred in November 1984, when 51-A recovered two stranded communications satellites. After recovering the second satellite, Dale Gardner celebrates in the payload bay by holding a sign reading "For Sale." The two satellites are in the bottom right corner of the picture.

and an external airlock was added, so that it could dock with the ISS when that was launched.

Discovery was removed from flight status in January 2002 to undergo Orbiter Maintenance and Modification (OMM) at KSC. The OMM began September 3, 2002, and was continuing through July 2003, when these words were written. The *Columbia* accident appears to have delayed completion of the OMM, as *Discovery* is not manifested for another flight through the end of 2004.

Despite this stand-down, *Discovery* has been in space more than any other Orbiter. *Discovery* flew 30 missions through 2003. It first flew on August 30, 1984, and completed five flights before the *Challenger* hiatus, including a military mission, 51-C. During that period it was used on four missions in one year, the only Orbiter to have reached that flight rate. *Discovery* was the Orbiter that flew the first post-*Challenger* mission, STS-26, in September 1988.

Discovery comes closest to becoming the "blue" or military Orbiter. It flew half the ten military missions flown by the Space Shuttle, and had been the Orbiter scheduled to fly the first two Vandenberg launches. It was also scheduled for the 61-N military flight, canceled after *Challenger*.

Discovery was manifested for two missions in September 1986 – both military: 62-B and 61-N. Whether this reflected a lack in confidence in SLC-6 being completed as scheduled or a preference for *Discovery* on military missions is hard to say. *Discovery* would have been used for the first two Vandenberg flights, and was one of two Orbiters capable of deploying the Centaur upper stage. Had the Shuttle program gone as planned, *Discovery* may have remained at Vandenberg, exclusively military in use.

Instead, along with *Atlantis*, *Discovery* remained at KSC to close out the Shuttle military program, and became one of the pillars of the space station program, making two trips to the Russian *Mir* and four trips to the ISS.

Early in its career, *Discovery* was used for one of the Shuttle program's greatest triumphs. Two communications satellites were stranded in useless orbits when their Payload Assist Module upper stages failed in February 1984. NASA devised a retrieval mission. Nine months later, in November 1984, *Discovery* was launched on mission 51-A, deployed two additional communications satellites, then rendezvoused with each stranded satellite, captured them, and returned them to Earth. Both were successfully relaunched. The mission was a showpiece for manned space travel. The capture device failed, so the crew improvised a capture method in real time.

Discovery also deployed the Hubble Space Telescope, the *Ulysses* interplanetary probe, and conducted three Spacelab/Spacehab missions, as well as conducting one HST (Hubble) servicing mission.

A camera on the launch pad support structure captures *Atlantis* as it lifts off for its first voyage to space, mission 51-J. *Atlantis* carried five crewmembers and two military satellites on the Shuttle's second Department of Defense mission.

OV-104 *Atlantis*

Atlantis, the fourth Orbiter completed, and the last intended for the fleet, was named after a two-masted sailing ketch used by the Woods Hole Oceanographic Institute in Massachusetts. This 460-ton vessel was used for oceanographic research from 1930 to 1966, the first American ship used for that purpose.

Atlantis was contracted in 1979 along with *Discovery*. Structural assembly began in March 1980, and was completed in April 1984. Although it took two months longer to complete than either *Columbia* or *Discovery*, the construction of *Atlantis* used 50 percent fewer man-hours, partly because the engineers applied lessons learned in the construction of the earlier vehicles. Like *Discovery*, *Atlantis* was completed with thermal blankets instead of silica tiles on much of the upper surfaces. Combined with other weight savings and structural improvements, *Atlantis* weighed 6,974lb less than *Columbia*,

Atlantis had its first OMDP between 1992 and 1994. During that 20-month refit, a drag chute was installed, the plumbing was altered so that it could fly extended missions, the airframe was modified, additional thermal protection was installed, and landing-gear door insulation was improved.

A second 10-month OMDP followed in 1998. An external airlock was installed in the payload bay so that *Atlantis* could dock with the ISS, the communications and cooling systems were improved, weight reduction measures were implemented, and the crew cabin floor strengthened. Additionally, *Atlantis* was the first Orbiter to receive the new "glass cockpit." Over 100 modifications were incorporated during this refit.

Atlantis first flew for 51-J, the second military mission, in October 1985. It flew only one other mission before the *Challenger* hiatus. *Atlantis* returned to space in December 1988 on STS-27, the second flight after the loss of *Challenger*, and another military mission. *Atlantis* flew two further military missions for a total of four.

Orbiter **_Atlantis_** **being mated to the 747 for transportation to KSC at the mate-demate device at Dryden Flight Research Center in 1991.**

Atlantis had flown 26 missions by the end of 2002, which included deployment of three significant planetary and space science satellites. In May 1989 it deployed the *Magellan Venus* probe on STS-30. Five months later, in October, it deployed *Galileo*, a planetary probe sent to Jupiter. Originally these were to have been launched using a Centaur upper stage, but the missions and satellites were modified to allow a solid fuel Inertial Upper Stage to be used. On April 7, 1992, *Atlantis* deployed the 34,000lb Compton Gamma Ray Observatory.

During STS-46, which launched July 31, 1992, *Atlantis* carried the Tethered Satellite System 1 (TSS-1), an ambitious joint US–Italian tethered satellite project. Unfortunately a problem with the reel prevented the satellite from deploying more than half a mile (860m) from *Atlantis*, and after three days of effort, the subsatellite was reeled in.

Atlantis also flew one stand-alone Spacelab flight in 1992, and seven missions where it rendezvoused and docked with the Russian *Mir* Space Station between 1995 and 1997. On those missions it used a Spacehab module to facilitate docking, and to provide additional working space.

During this program, *Atlantis* conducted the first astronaut shuttles of the Space Shuttle program, where a crew person was left at *Mir* on one mission to be retrieved and exchanged for a replacement on a later mission. This flight finally validated the concept of using the Space Shuttle as a space station resupply vehicle, an ambition which had been part of NASA's initial motivation to build a space shuttle in the late 1960s.

Since completing its 1998 overhaul, *Atlantis* has been used exclusively for the construction and supply of the ISS. As of December 2002, *Atlantis* made six flights to the ISS, carrying supplies and structural elements to assemble the ISS.

OV-105 *Endeavour*

Endeavour, the fifth and final Orbiter to fly in space, is named for the ship HMS *Endeavour* (formerly a collier) commanded by Captain James Cook on his first voyage of exploration, 1768–71. The name was chosen from those submitted in a national competition open to United States students in primary and secondary schools.

Like its namesake, the Orbiter *Endeavour* is a conversion. With the closure of the Orbiter production line after the completion of *Atlantis*, NASA needed spares to provide replacement parts for damaged elements. NASA issued a supplementary contract to Rockwell International in April 1983 for an aft-fuselage, crew compartment, mid-fuselage, forward fuselage halves, vertical tail and rudder, wings, elevons, forward RCS, one set of OMS/RCS pods, and a body flap.

At the time of the *Challenger* accident, the mid-fuselage and the body flap had been completed and were in storage. Construction of several other parts was also well advanced (work on the crew module had begun in 1982 – before the structural spares contract had been signed). On July 31, 1987 NASA awarded Rockwell International a contract to build a replacement Orbiter – OV-105 – using the structural spares. Rockwell reactivated the assembly floor at their Palmdale facility on August 3, and fabrication of OV-105 began in September.

Endeavour was completed on July 6, 1990, and delivered to NASA on April 25, 1991. The completed Orbiter was a prototype for improvements the other Orbiters would receive in subsequent out-of-service overhauls. It had a drag parachute, plumbing and electrical connections that would permit 28-day missions, upgraded avionics, nose-wheel steering, and improved APUs (Auxiliary Power Units).

ABOVE ***Endeavour* approaches ISS with a truss package. The new, external airlock is visible immediately behind the crew cabin. The dish immediately to the right of the crew cabin is the rendezvous radar.**

Endeavour underwent an eight-month OMDP in 1996 and 1997, where an external airlock was added so it could support the ISS program.

Endeavour flew its first mission, STS-49, on May 7, 1992, demonstrating the post-*Challenger* capabilities for the first time. The mission included a dramatic satellite rescue. Ironically, the satellite they captured, INTELSAT VI, had been stranded by a failure of a Titan expendable launch vehicle, to which many such satellites had been shifted after the *Challenger* hiatus.

Endeavour flew 19 missions prior to the *Columbia* accident in February 2003. Unique among the Orbiters, it never flew, or was scheduled for a military mission. By the time it joined the fleet, the Defense Department had abandoned the Shuttle for military purposes.

It also only deployed one payload with an upper stage intended to take it to a higher orbit, a TDRSS on STS-54 in 1993. This reflects the change in use of the Shuttle following *Challenger*, with less emphasis on its use as a satellite delivery system. Instead, *Endeavour* has carried a number of Spacelab/Spacehab payloads, as well as deploying then retrieving a number of free-flying research satellites, such as Spartan, EURICA, and the Wake Shield Unit. Additionally, *Endeavour* conducted the first commercial Spacehab mission, on STS-77 in 1996.

Endeavour also carried out the Hubble Space Telescope (HST) repair mission in 1993. This involved several long space walks to correct serious problems with the HST imaging system. *Endeavour* docked with *Mir* on one mission, and since 1999 has supported construction of the ISS, carrying elements or supplies to the ISS on six missions.

BELOW **The External Tank photographed drifting back to Earth after a successful ascent in 2002.**

ACRONYMS

ADI Attitude Director Indicator
ADS Air Data System
AFB Air Force Base
ALT Approach and Landing Test
AOA Abort Once Around (Shuttle abort mode)
APU Auxiliary Power Unit
ATCS Active Thermal Control System
ATO Abort To Orbit (Shuttle abort mode)
BFS Backup Flight System (Shuttle backup computer)
C&T Communications and Tracking
C/W Caution and Warning
c.g. Center of gravity
COAS Crewman Optical Alignment Sight
CPU Central Processor Unit
CRT Cathode Ray Tube
DAP Digital Autopilot
DOD, DoD Department of Defense
EAFB Edwards Air Force Base
ECLSS Environmental control and life support system
ELV Expendable Launch Vehicle
EMU Extravehicular mobility unit
EPS Electrical Power System
ESA European Space Agency
ET External Tank
EVA Extravehicular Activity
FM Frequency Modulation, Frequency Modulated
fps Feet per second
GN&C Guidance, Navigation and Control
GMT Greenwich Mean Time
GPC General-Purpose Computer (Shuttle onboard computer)
GPS Global Positioning System (constellation of satellites in a 12-hr orbit used for navigation)
HAC Heading Alignment Cylinder
HSI Horizontal Situation Indicator
HST Hubble Space Telescope
HUD Heads-Up Display
IMU Inertial Measurement Unit
ISS International Space Station
ITA Integrated Test Article
IUS Inertial Upper Stage
JPL Jet Propulsion Laboratory
JSC Johnson Space Center
KSC Kennedy Space Center
LDEF Long Duration Exposure Facility (satellite carrying small payloads to examine effects of space environment, left in orbit to be retrieved on a future flight)
LH2 Liquid Hydrogen
LO2 Liquid Oxygen
LRU Line-Replaceable Unit
MDD Mate/Demate Device
MDM Multiplexer/demultiplexer
MECO Main engine cutoff
MET Mission Elapsed Time
MMH Monomethyl Hydrazine
MMU Manned Maneuvering Unit
MOL Manned Orbiting Laboratory (DOD reconnaissance station)
MPS Main Propulsion System (Shuttle main engines)
MPTA Main Propulsion Test Article
MSBLS Microwave Scan Beam Landing System
MSFC Marshall Space Flight Center
NASA National Aeronautics and Space Administration
NSTL National Space Technology Laboratory
nmi Nautical mile
N_2O_4 Nitrogen Tetroxide
OMS Orbital Maneuvering System (Shuttle secondary engines)
OV Orbiter Vehicle
PAM Payload Assist Module
PASS Primary Avionics Software System (Shuttle onboard computer software)
PBI Push Button Indicator
PEAP Personal Egress Air Pack (emergency oxygen)
PLB Payload Bay (the major mission payloads were stored here)
PLBD Payload Bay Doors
psi Pounds per square inch
RA Radar Altimeter
RCC Reinforced Carbon-Carbon (thermal protection on leading edge and other high-heat areas)
RCS Reaction Control System (Orbiter maneuvering jets)
RGA Rate Gyro Assembly
RHC Rotational Hand Controller (pilot's controller used on Orbiter for attitude control)
RMS Remote Manipulator System (Orbiter robot arm)
RTLS Return To Launch Site (Shuttle abort mode)
SAIL Shuttle Avionics Integration Laboratory (JSC)
SCA Shuttle Carrier Aircraft (747 that ferries the Orbiter)
Scramjet Supersonic Combustion RAMJET (a hypersonic ramjet engine that burns its fuel externally, in the supersonic airstream produced by an aircraft)
SLC-6 Space Launch Complex 6
SRB Solid Rocket Booster
SRM Solid Rocket Motor (motors on SRBs)
SSME Space Shuttle Main Engine (Shuttle primary engines)
ST Star Tracker
STA Structural Test Article
STDN Spaceflight Tracking and Data Network (communications & tracking system)
STS Space Transportation System
T/W Thrust-to-weight
TACAN Tactical air navigation
TAEM Terminal Area Energy Management (Landing regime)
TDRS Tracking and Data Relay Satellite (communications and tracking satellite used with Shuttle)
TDRSS Tracking and Data Relay Satellite system (the system, including ground tracking stations used with the TDRS satellites)
THC Translational hand controller (pilot's controller used on Orbiter for translation)
TIO Target insertion orbit
TPS Thermal protection system (system used to keep Orbiter from melting during reentry)
TVC Thrust vector control
UHF Ultrahigh frequency
VAB Vehicle Assembly Building
VAFB Vandenberg Air Force Base
WSTF White Sands Test Facility

SHUTTLE MISSION NUMBERING SYSTEM

Shuttle missions used one of two numbering systems.

STS-n: STS stands for Space Transportation System. The number that follows (eg: STS-105) is the order in which the mission was manifested for flight. NASA used this system for the first nine Shuttle flights and all Shuttle flights after the *Challenger* hiatus. Since numbering is assigned as flights are manifested, sometimes missions fly out of sequence. STS-107, the flight on which *Columbia* was lost, was delayed. As a result, this flight, the 113th Shuttle mission, flew after STS-111, STS-112, and STS-113. While the next flight after the *Columbia* hiatus will be STS-114 (and will be the 114th Shuttle flight), the flight manifested to fly after that is STS-121, which was manifested during the *Columbia* hiatus, and after STS-115 through 120 were planned.

41-G: The first number represents the fiscal year in which the mission was manifested to fly. A flight starting with a "4" was originally scheduled to fly sometime in Fiscal Year 1984. (A fiscal year for the United States Federal Government starts on October 1 of the previous year, and ends on September 30 of the year. FY1984 started on October 1, 1983, and ended September 30, 1984.) The second number represents the launch site: 1 is the Kennedy Space Center; 2 is Vandenberg AFB. The letter represents the order in which the flight was manifested in the fiscal year. "A" was the first flight, "L" was the 12th. Occasionally you will see missions referenced as STS-41G instead of 41-G, even at NASA. This is anachronistic, a practice occasionally seen after NASA went back to the STS numbering system with STS-26.

So 51-L (when *Challenger* was destroyed) was originally manifested to fly in FY1985 (between Oct 1984 and Sept 1985) from KSC (the 1), and was the 12th flight scheduled for FY1985. Schedule problems often shifted the order in which flights were made. Flight 51-B flew after 51-C and 51-D. Missions 51-E and 51-H were never flown. Flight 51-L was launched in January 1986, well after the end of FY1985, and after missions 61-A, 61-B, and 61-C.

CORPORATE IDENTITIES

Over the 30-plus years of the Shuttle program many of the manufacturers involved have changed names or been purchased by other companies. This list is not exhaustive, but does attempt to list the major changes.

North American Aviation (built the Apollo capsule and X-15) was purchased by **Rockwell**, and became **North American Rockwell**. In the late 1970s **Rockwell** abandoned the North American name becoming **Rockwell International**. In the 1990s **Boeing** purchased **Rockwell**, and the company is now known as **Boeing**. **Boeing** (built the Saturn V first stage) has remained Boeing throughout, even after absorbing **McDonnell Douglas** and **Rockwell**.

Douglas Aircraft and **Aerospace** (built Skylab) was purchased by **McDonnell Aircraft** (Mercury and Gemini capsules) in the late 1960s, becoming **McDonnell-Douglas**. In the late 1990s, **McDonnell Douglas** merged with **Boeing**, and the resulting company was known as **Boeing**.

Lockheed (manufactured many unmanned satellites) purchased **General Dynamics** in the early 1990s, using the **Lockheed** name. Then **Lockheed** and **Martin-Marietta** (manufactured the Titian booster) merged in 1995 as **Lockheed-Martin**.

Grumman (built the Lunar Module) merged with **Northrop** (B-2 bomber) to form **Northrop-Grumman**.

Spacelab was set of ESA science modules built for and flown on the Shuttle. **Spacehab** was a US company that licensed **Spacelab** technology from the ESA and built a commercial science module that has also flown on the Shuttle. **Spacehab** has since build modules for the ISS.

BIBLIOGRAPHY

Allaway, Howard, *The Space Shuttle At Work*, SP-432, Scientific and Technical Information Branch and Division of Public Affairs, National Aeronautics and Space Administration, Washington, D.C. 1979

Guillemette, Roger, "The curse of Slick Six, Fact or fiction?" *Florida Today*, May 10, 1999.

Heppenheimer, T. A., *The Space Shuttle Decision: NASA's Search for a Reusable Space Vehicle*, NASA SP-4221, NASA History Series, National Aeronautics and Space Administration, Washington, D.C. 1999.

Logsdon, John M. (Ed.), *Exploring the Unknown. Selected Documents in the History of the U.S. Civil Space Program. Volume 4: Accessing Space*, NASA SP-4407, NASA/Superintendent of Documents, Washington, D.C. 1999.

Mission Operations Directorate, *Space Shuttle Vehicle Familiarization*, TD346, Space Flight Training & Facility Operations, Shuttle Systems Training Branch, Johnson Space Center, Houston, TX, December 2000.

NASA Fact Sheet, *The 21st Century Shuttle*, FS-2000-03-010-JSC, Johnson Space Center, Houston, TX 2000

Oberg, James E., *Space Power Theory*, US Government Printing Office, Washington, D.C. 1999

Oberg, James E., *Star-Crossed Orbits. Inside the U.S.-Russian Space Alliance*, McGraw-Hill, New York, 2002.

Oberg, James E., *Towards a Theory of Space Power*, Washington Round Table on Science and Public Policy, The George C. Marshall Institute, Washington, D.C., 2003.

Shuttle Operational Data Book, NSTS-08934, Revision E, Lyndon B. Johnson Space Center, Houston, TX, January 1988.

Wade, Mark, editor, *Encyclopedia Astronautica*, http://www.astronautix.com/, 2003.

Websites

The SLC-6 Saga, http://www.fas.org/spp/military/program/launch/sts_slc-6.htm, Federation of American Scientists, 1999.

NSTS 1998 News Reference Manual, http://science.ksc.nasa.gov/shuttle/technology/sts-newsref/, Kennedy Space Center, FL, 1998.

Past Shuttle Missions, http://spaceflight.nasa.gov/shuttle/archives/index.html, NASA Headquarters, Washington, DC, 2003.

Shuttle Mission Archive, http://www-pao.ksc.nasa.gov/kscpao/shuttle/missions/missions.html, Kennedy Space Center, FL, 2003.

Shuttle Operational Data Book, online version, http://spaceflight.nasa.gov/shuttle/reference/sodb/, NASA Headquarters, Washington, DC, 2003

Shuttle Image Gallery, http://spaceflight.nasa.gov/gallery/images/shuttle/, NASA Headquarters, Washington, DC, 2003.

COLOR PLATE COMMENTARY

A: PROFILES OF ORBITERS

Each Orbiter is unique, and most differences are internal. The major external difference is in the tile patterns: *Columbia* and *Challenger* had tiles on the outer upper wings and upper forward fuselage, whereas *Atlantis*, *Discovery*, and *Endeavour* substituted thermal blankets. *Enterprise* (not shown in the plate) lacked thermal tiles, had a different nose shape, and an air-data probe in the nose.

NASA adopted the main color scheme shown by *Discovery* on this plate in 1998. The four surviving Orbiters were repainted to match this scheme during either OMDPs or OMM periods that year. Prior to that, Orbiters' markings varied. All had the United State Flag, with the words "United States" on the sides, and the NASA 'worm" logo on the payload bay doors just forward of the OMS pods. (NASA replaced its blue and red "meatball," in 1976. A stylized set of initials substituted as a logo until 1993, when the "meatball" was restored.)

Enterprise and *Columbia* (as shown by *Columbia* on this plate), initially had a US flag on the upper left wing, and "USA" in block black initials on the right wing, with the name of the Orbiter, printed in black, on the payload bay doors, immediately aft of the front. While receiving maintenance during the *Challenger* hiatus, *Colombia* had the name moved to the forebody, under the side window, but markings were otherwise unchanged.

Between 1981 and 1998 the rest of the Orbiter fleet used the following markings. The Orbiter's name was on the forebody, beneath the side window. As shown by *Challenger*, the rest of the Orbiters were painted so that the left upper wing had the letters "USA" in black, with the United States flag immediately below it. The right upper wing had the NASA crawl logo, in dark gray, with the vehicle name immediately below. At some point prior to the SLC-6 fit tests in 1986, *Enterprise*'s wing markings were altered to match the rest of the fleet.

B: STS-1 LAUNCH

The first Shuttle mission launched into space on April 12, 1981, after many frustrating delays. In January 1981 a gag calendar circulated around Johnson Space Center repeating the Center Director's proclamation: "We *Will* Launch in March!" Every month between February and December was labeled March. Some veterans of that era joke that *Columbia* was launched on March 43rd.

This Orbiter is *Columbia*, although its unique wing markings cannot be seen from this bird's eye view. The white External Tank marks an early launch and identifies the Orbiter as *Columbia*. The tank's insulation is brown, although initially it was painted white, for thermal control. The paint weighed nearly 500lb and as the ET is carried most of the way to orbit, an unpainted tank increased payload by almost the weight of the tank. NASA soon decided that the thermal qualities of a white tank were less important than payload. After STS-2 the tanks were left unpainted in the brown that has become a signature of the Shuttle program.

The Shuttle has cleared the launch tower in the plate. The Shuttle's thrust-to-weight ratio is 1.5:1, compared to 1.2:1 for the earlier Saturn V. Those that watched both lift off often comment on the speed at which the Shuttle departs, compared to the more stately progress of a Saturn V. STS-1 marked the first launch from Launch Complex 39 since the last Saturn launch on July 17, 1975. The Apollo launch crawlers were used, and the pad was extensively modified for the Shuttle program.

In the Vehicle Assembly Building, *Discovery* is being lifted in preparation to being mated with the External Tank for STS-95.

C: FLIGHT DECK/COCKPIT

Anyone who flies aircraft would recognize the instrument layout in the Shuttle forward cockpit. It was the first spacecraft to use an instrument panel laid out like an aircraft's. In front of both the commander and pilot is a panel with the familiar "T" of flight control instruments – or rather the spacefaring equivalents.

Instead of an airspeed indicator in the top left is an Alpha/Mach Indicator that indicates angle of attack, acceleration and Mach number. In the center-top, the artificial horizon is replaced by an Attitude Direction Indicator, or "eight-ball." Instead of an altimeter on the upper left, the Orbiter has an altitude/Vertical Velocity Indicator. Where the compass sits on an airplane, the Orbiter uses a Horizontal Situation Indicator.

During landing, when the Orbiter reenters like an airplane, these controls behave like their aircraft analogs. On orbit they measure acceleration, attitude and attitude rates.

The Orbiter originally had three CRT displays positioned between the commander and pilot, used for displaying information. The top half of the plate illustrates the original configuration – as modified with the Heads-Up Display (HUD) used during entry. The CRTs display a wide range of data formats to present information critical to the mission activities being undertaken.

In 1998, NASA began replacing this design with a "glass cockpit" shown in the lower half of the plate, whereby flat panels display the flight instruments digitally. The displays in the center of the panel were increased from three green-screen CRTs to five full-color flat panel displays. In addition to increasing the flexibility with which data could be displayed, the new cockpit requires less electrical power and weighs 75lb less than the original instrument panel. *Atlantis* was the first Orbiter to receive the modified panel, followed by *Columbia*. *Discovery* is being modified in 2003, but *Endeavour* may not receive these upgrades until 2006.

The cockpit of *Enterprise* immediately prior to the fifth and final ALT free flight. Fred Haise, an Apollo-13 veteran, commanded the flight in the left seat. Gordon Fullerton, a former MOL astronaut was the pilot.

D: CUTAWAY OF SHUTTLE STACK

The Space Shuttle has three major parts – an Orbiter, one External Tank and two Solid Rocket Boosters.

The winged Orbiter carries the crew and payload. It glides to a dead-stick landing to conclude a successful mission. It contains the most expensive parts of the systems – life support systems, the main engines that put the Shuttle in orbit, the Remote Manipulator System (the Shuttle's robot arm), avionics, and computers.

The Space Shuttle main engines exhaust 8hrs 30mins after launch. Limited orbital changes are then done with the Orbital Maneuvering System (OMS), two engines with 6,000lb thrust mounted in pods on the back of the Orbiter. Orbiter attitude is maintained with the Reaction Control System (RCS). The RCS has two aft modules on each OMS pod and a forward RCS module. Six RCS jets are vernier thrusters generating 24lb of thrust. The rest, 38 Primary jets, each produce 870lb of thrust. OMS and RCS use storable propellants, liquid at room temperature, that spontaneously combust when the oxydizer mixes with the fuel. The OMS engines and the aft RCS are interconnected. The Orbiter could deorbit with just the RCS jets, if necessary.

The External Tank, the largest element of the stack, contains tanks for liquid hydrogen and liquid oxygen, and an intertank section that connects the oxygen tank in the nose of the ET with the hydrogen tank in the main body of the ET. The intertank also contains a structural beam that holds the SRBs during ascent. The ET is the only disposable part of the Shuttle and normally crashes in the Indian Ocean after launch.

Two Solid Rocket Boosters provide the first-stage thrust for the Shuttle. When the SRBs exhaust, they fall away from the Shuttle and parachute back to earth, where they are recovered.

The Orbiter is controlled in space with using a 44-jet Reaction Control System. Here, two aft primary RCS jets can be seen firing.

E: SRB SEP (SEPARATION)

Watch the crowd in a film of a Shuttle launch. If they cheer when the Shuttle clears the launch tower, the launch was filmed before the *Challenger* accident. If they cheer at SRB separation, 126 seconds after launch, it was filmed after *Challenger*.

SRB separation represents a milestone. Once the solid rocket motors ignite, the Shuttle is committed to flight until the SRBs burn out. If all three SSMEs failed at SRB ignition, the SRBs alone will lift the Shuttle off the pad.

When combustion chamber pressure in both SRBs drop below 50psi, the flight software initiates the SRB separation. The pressure limit ensures that both SRBs have burned out prior to separation, and that they will not swing in, striking the ET.

The forward ET attachment is a ball and socket; the SRB has the ball, and a pin with an explosive bolt connects the ball to the SRB. The aft SRB attachment is composed of three struts with an explosive bolt at each end. When SRB Sep is initiated, the bolts are detonated (see inset), freeing the SRBs from the External Tank.

There are four booster separation motors on each end of each SRB. After the bolts have blown, the motors are ignited, pushing the SRBs away from the ET and Orbiter. The nose, pushed by the airstream, falls away more quickly, and the Shuttle's onboard computers switch control to the Orbiter's rate gyro assemblies.

As the SRBs fall, the nose cone pops off at 15,700ft, as sensed by a barometric altimeter. A ribbon parachute first slows the SRB, then three main parachutes deploy, slowing the fall so the SRB can be recovered at sea.

F: LANDING

One of the most visible changes adopted after *Challenger* was the addition of a drag parachute to slow the Orbiter without additional braking. The parachute is stored in a compartment at the base of the tail. It is deployed after the Orbiter has landed on the runway, normally after the nose wheel has touched down. The drag chute is then dropped before the Orbiter stops to prevent it from interfering with the vehicles that service the Orbiter after landing.

The drag chute has the potential to reduce the post-landing rollout by 1,000–2,000ft, significantly reducing the runway length requirements. However, the drag chute does not necessarily reduce the Orbiter's rollout distance – the distance between the point at which the Orbiter's main wheel touches the ground and the point at which it stops. Rather, it eases loads on the brakes. In turn, this reduces

An External Tank under assembly in what was then the *Martin Marietta Aerospace* factory in Michoud, LA. Today, this plant is run by Lockheed-Martin.

brake friction heating which reduces the chances of a tire bursting during landing.

The plate illustrates the first use of the drag parachute, at the end of Shuttle mission STS-49, in 1992, *Endeavour*'s maiden voyage. The drag chute was retrofitted on the existing Orbiters during 1992. On STS-49, *Endeavour* landed at Edwards Air Force Base in California, touching down on Runway 22, the paved runway used for Shuttle landings. Rollout was 9,490ft. While longer than the shortest rollout (6,364ft on STS-37 in 1991), it is shorter than the 13,732-ft rollout concluding STS-3, the only Shuttle flight that landed at White Sands, New Mexico.

A Shuttle night landing on KSC Runway 15 concludes STS-72 on January 20, 1996. The lights in the centers of the SSME and OMS engine bells are from light reflecting off the ignition chambers.

G: HST REPAIR

The Hubble Space Telescope, launched from the Shuttle in April, 1990, was one of the first satellites designed with the intention of using the Space Shuttle for servicing. It included items not carried on earlier research satellites, such as trunnions to allow the HST to be grasped by the Shuttle RMS, handholds and footholds for astronauts to ease servicing activities, and modular components that could be extracted and replaced in space.

The servicing capability prevented the Hubble from becoming the world's most expensive opera glasses. A manufacturing error, undiscovered until it was in orbit, prevented the telescope from focusing properly. This precluded its use for many optical purposes. The problem was repaired on a subsequent Shuttle mission, and the HST has since given humans glimpses into the cosmos impossible to see from Earth.

NASA has flown a total of four repair and servicing missions through January 2003. A final visit is tentatively scheduled for 2005, but might be canceled given safety concerns that have emerged since the loss of *Columbia*.

The most recent HST servicing mission, STS-109, was flown in March 2002. During that mission, a power unit and HST's solar panels were replaced, and a reaction wheel assembly (for attitude control) and a new camera were installed.

The plate shows the HST being released after the end of the servicing it received during that mission. The Hubble now sports smaller, yet more efficient solar panels, which replaced the gold-colored panels with which the HST was launched. Additionally, two members of the STS-109 crew, payload commander John M. Grunsfeld and mission specialist Richard M. Linnehan installed a new Power Control Unit on the satellite.

INDEX